AQA History

AS Unit 1

Britain, 1906–1951

Exclusively endorsed by AQA

Chris Collier

Chris Rowe

Series editor
Sally Waller

Nelson Thornes

Published in 2008 by:
Nelson Thornes Ltd
Delta Place
27 Bath Road
CHELTENHAM
GL53 7TH
United Kingdom

09 10 11 12 / 10 9 8 7 6 5 4 3

A catalogue record for this book is available from the British Library

978-0-7487-8262-8

Illustrations by David Russell Illustration and Bob Moulder (c/o Graham-Cameron Illustration)

Page make-up by Thomson Digital

Printed and bound in China by 1010 Printing International Ltd

Contents

AQA introduction

Nelson Thornes and AQA

Nelson Thornes has worked in collaboration with AQA to ensure that this book offers you the best support for your AS or A level course and helps you to prepare for your exams. The partnership means that you can be confident that the range of learning, teaching and assessment practice materials has been checked by the senior examining team at AQA before formal approval, and is closely matched to the requirements of your specification.

How to use this book

This book covers the specification for your course and is arranged in a sequence approved by AQA.

The features in this book include:

Timeline

Key events are outlined at the beginning of the book. The events are colour-coded so you can clearly see the categories of change.

Learning objectives

At the beginning of each section you will find a list of learning objectives that contain targets linked to the requirements of the specification.

Key chronology

A short list of dates usually with a focus on a specific event or legislation.

Key profile

The profile of a key person you should be aware of to fully understand the period in question.

Key term

A term that you will need to be able to define and understand.

Did you know?

Interesting information to bring the subject under discussion to life.

Exploring the detail

Information to put further context around the subject under discussion.

A closer look

An in-depth look at a theme, person or event to deepen your understanding. Activities around the extra information may be included.

Sources

Sources to reinforce topics or themes and may provide fact or opinion. They may be quotations from historical works, contemporaries of the period or photographs.

Cross-reference

Links to related content within the book which may offer more detail on the subject in question.

Activity

Various activity types to provide you with different challenges and opportunities to demonstrate both the content and skills you are learning. Some can be worked on individually, some as part of group work and some are designed to specifically 'stretch and challenge'.

Table 1 *Unit 1: style of questions and marks available*

Unit 1	Question	Marks	Question type	Question stem	Hints for students
Question 1, 2 and 3	(a)	12	This question is focused on a narrow issue within the period studied and requires an explanation	Why did… Explain why… In what ways… (was X important)	Make sure you explain 'why', not 'how', and try to order your answer in a way that shows you understand the inter-linkage of factors and which were the more important. You should try to reach an overall judgement/conclusion
Question 1, 2 and 3	(b)	24	This question links the narrow issue to a wider context and requires an awareness that issues and events can have different interpretations	How far… How important was… How successful…	This answer needs to be planned as you will need to develop an argument in your answer and show balanced judgement. Try to set out your argument in the introduction and, as you develop your ideas through your paragraphs, support your opinions with detailed evidence. Your conclusion should flow naturally and provide supported judgement

Marking criteria

Question 1(a), 2(a) and 3(a)

Level 1 Answers will contain either some descriptive material that is only loosely linked to the focus of the question or some explicit comment with little, if any, appropriate support. Answers are likely to be generalised and assertive. The response will be limited in development and skills of written communication will be weak. *(0–2 marks)*

Level 2 Answers will demonstrate some knowledge and understanding of the demands of the question. They will **either** be almost entirely descriptive with few explicit links to the question **or** they will provide some explanations backed by evidence that is limited in range and/or depth. Answers will be coherent but weakly expressed and/or poorly structured. *(3–6 marks)*

Level 3 Answers will demonstrate good understanding of the demands of the question providing relevant explanations backed by appropriately selected information, although this may not be full or comprehensive. Answers will, for the most part, be clearly expressed and show some organisation in the presentation of material. *(7–9 marks)*

Level 4 Answers will be well focused, identifying a range of specific explanations backed by precise evidence and demonstrating good understanding of the connections and links between events/issues. Answers will, for the most part, be well written and organised. *(10–12 marks)*

Question 1(b), 2(b) and 3(b)

Level 1 Answers may **either** contain some descriptive material which is only loosely linked to the focus of the question **or** they may address only a part of the question. Alternatively, there may be some explicit comment with little, if any, appropriate support. Answers are likely to be generalised and assertive. There will be little, if any, awareness of differing historical interpretations. The response will be limited in development and skills of written communication will be weak. *(0–6 marks)*

Level 2 Answers will show some understanding of the focus of the question. They will **either** be almost entirely descriptive with few explicit links to the question **or** they may contain some explicit comment with relevant but limited support. They will display limited understanding of differing historical interpretations. Answers will be coherent but weakly expressed and/or poorly structured. *(7–11 marks)*

Level 3 Answers will show a developed understanding of the demands of the question. They will provide some assessment, backed by relevant and appropriately selected evidence, but they will lack depth and/or balance. There will be some understanding of varying historical interpretations. Answers will, for the most part, be clearly expressed and show some organisation in the presentation of material. *(12–16 marks)*

Level 4 Answers will show explicit understanding of the demands of the question. They will develop a balanced argument backed by a good range of appropriately selected evidence and a good understanding of historical interpretations. Answers will, for the most part, show organisation and good skills of written communication. *(17–21 marks)*

Level 5 Answers will be well focused and closely argued. The arguments will be supported by precisely selected evidence leading to a relevant conclusion/judgement, incorporating well-developed understanding of historical interpretations and debate. Answers will, for the most part, be carefully organised and fluently written, using appropriate vocabulary. *(22–24 marks)*

Introduction to this book

At the beginning of the 20th century a British citizen might have been forgiven for believing that he or she lived in the richest and most powerful country in the world. Britain was the world's greatest trading nation and lay at the centre of an empire covering almost a quarter of the globe. In the second half of the 19th century, millions of people left Britain as emigrants – mainly to the United States, Canada, Australia, New Zealand and South Africa. The city of London was the heart of world banking, finance and investment. Britain was a leading industrial nation building 60 per cent of the world's merchant ships and supplying much of the world's textiles, machinery, iron and steel. The Royal Navy guarded both Britain and its worldwide empire and was larger than the navies of any other two nations put together.

In 1906, the United Kingdom of Great Britain and Ireland had a population of 43 million. Most British workers were employed in industry: textiles in Leeds, Bradford and Lancashire; coal mining in South Wales, Yorkshire and the north east; shipbuilding in Liverpool, Glasgow and Belfast; engineering in Birmingham and the West Midlands; and steel in Sheffield. A 'North–South divide' already existed. Agriculture now accounted for only a small proportion of the workforce. Employment was, however, increasing both for men and women in services such as retailing, transport, banking and education. Domestic service as maids, cooks and gardeners was the biggest single category of occupation in 1906, especially for women. New industries such as electricity, chemicals and motor cars were also being established by 1906, but they were not yet fully developed.

Although Britain was a great empire and an industrial giant, there were serious underlying problems. Britain's industrial and commercial supremacy was being challenged. By 1906, the United States and Germany had overtaken Britain in manufacturing. There were also stark contrasts between wealth and poverty. A third of the national income went to 3 per cent of the population; 10 per cent of the people owned 90 per cent of the country's wealth. At the other extreme, there was desperate poverty. Some 4 million people lived at or below subsistence level largely as a result of low wages, irregular employment, illness or old age.

Some of the anxieties about British society had been intensified by the experiences of the South African, or Boer, War of 1899–1902. The war in South Africa against 60,000 'Boers' (Dutch-speaking settlers) had exposed serious military failings and dented national self-confidence. The army had also been alarmed to discover the poor physical condition of huge numbers of the working-class men called up to fight. Government reports into the problems raised concerns about poor health and the impact of poverty and malnutrition.

Not surprisingly, there was also a growing demand for social and political reform. Living conditions in the poorest areas were appalling. Educational opportunities were still limited for the vast majority. Women and many men did not yet have the right to vote in parliamentary elections. England dominated the United Kingdom but in Wales, Scotland and above all in

Fig. 1 *Pomp and Circumstance. Edward VII, king from 1901–10, pays a visit to Newcastle in 1906. His mother, Queen Victoria, reigned for 63 years, and Edward had to wait until he was 59 to become king*

■ **Key term**

Parliamentary monarchy: although great constitutional powers remained with the sovereign – King Edward VII in 1906 – these were exercised by the prime minister and his cabinet who were responsible to parliament and ultimately to the voters for their policies. Parliament in 1906 consisted of an elected House of Commons and an unelected House of Lords.

Ireland, there were demands for greater influence over their national affairs. By 1906, movements were already underway to remedy some of these injustices.

During the 19th century, Britain had become a largely industrial nation, with a massive shift in population from the countryside to large towns and cities. Despite these changes, Britain's political system of **parliamentary monarchy** remained remarkably stable. Unlike many European countries or even the United States, Britain had not experienced revolution or civil war in the 19th century. Men's right to vote had been widened in 1832, 1867 and 1884. Working people had founded trade unions to protect their interests, and new political parties had emerged. At the beginning of the 20th century, Britain seemed to be a model democracy. Nevertheless, politicians and political parties faced a whole series of controversial domestic issues at the beginning of the 20th century – poverty, trade unionism, democracy and, in Ireland, Nationalism. Four political parties represented the voters in the United Kingdom parliament at Westminster, though only two of these were capable of forming a government in their own right in 1906.

■ The political parties to 1906

The Conservative Party

The Conservative Party was often referred to as the Unionist Party, because it was associated with fighting Home Rule and keeping Ireland in the Union. (In 1886, Home Rule for Ireland had split the Liberals, with many Liberal Unionists joining the Conservatives – hence the title 'Conservative and Unionist Party'). On the whole, the Conservatives were seen as the party of the great landowners, of the Church of England and of big business. Since the 1870s, however, the Conservatives had also been winning support amongst the middle and working classes and by 1900 more Conservative MPs had a background in industry, trade and the professions.

Between 1886 and 1906, the Conservatives won three of the four general elections and formed the government for 17 years out of 20. They also had an overwhelming majority of seats in the House of Lords. Support for the Conservatives was strong, not only in rural areas but also in the industrial towns and cities, such as Sheffield, Manchester and Birmingham.

Various factors help to explain this Conservative dominance. Lord Salisbury, Conservative leader from 1885 until 1901, skilfully exploited the Liberal split over Home Rule. He promoted limited reforms in government such as the introduction of elected county councils in 1888 and free elementary schooling in 1891 in order to satisfy some of the demands of the Liberal Unionists. When the Liberal Party was briefly in power between 1892 and 1895, Salisbury used the Unionist majority in the House of Lords to frustrate their programme, for example by blocking Gladstone's renewed attempt to bring in Home Rule for Ireland.

Key profiles

Lord Salisbury

Robert Cecil, Lord Salisbury, was leader of the Conservative Party and prime minister, in 1885–6, 1886–92, 1895–1900 and 1900–2. As an aristocrat, he was the last prime minister to govern from the House of Lords. He was particularly interested in foreign affairs and often combined the post of Foreign Secretary with that of prime minister. Salisbury was shrewd enough to understand the need for the Conservative Party to adapt to social change, although, despite some useful rural and local government reforms, he neglected urban social reform.

William Ewart Gladstone

Gladstone was a giant figure in the Liberal Party and was prime minister four times between 1868 and 1894. He was a famous orator and moral crusader who saw himself and his party as key to progress and reform – but his career ended in failure because of the divisive issue of Home Rule for Ireland. All Gladstone's attempts to pass a Home Rule bill failed; and the Liberal Party was hopelessly split in 1886. After Gladstone's death, the Liberals began to move away from Gladstonian ideas towards the 'New Liberalism'.

Social changes, especially the growth of a lower middle class of clerical workers, shopkeepers, teachers, foremen and junior managers, benefited the Conservatives. These groups aspired to be property owners, perhaps buying a house in the new suburbs. The Conservative leadership set out to win support from 'Villa Toryism' by targeting such voters in their speeches, through organisations like the **Primrose League**. The Primrose League enabled the Conservatives to give these male voters, and especially their wives, a role in the local party and a chance to mix with higher social groups.

The Conservatives were also able to attract some support amongst the working classes. In rural areas this was due to deference towards traditional landowning families such as the Earl of Derby in west Lancashire. However, the Conservatives also had considerable working-class support in the urban areas of counties like Lancashire. Partly this was because Lancashire cotton mill-owners traditionally supported the Liberals and so their workers voted **Tory**. In cities such as Liverpool and Glasgow, support for the Conservatives was based on opposition to immigrants, primarily the Irish who were seen as taking jobs and lowering wages. There was sometimes an unpleasant sectarian edge to local politics. The Conservatives also attracted support by projecting an image of patriotism and of pride in empire and by 'standing up' for British interests abroad. In 1900, the Conservatives exploited the expected victory over the Boers by calling and winning the 'khaki' election. But their political dominance was not only down to Conservative strengths; it was also due to the weaknesses of their opponents.

The Liberal Party

The Liberal Party was the other leading party in British politics before 1906. Liberalism was founded on an alliance between **Whig** aristocrats,

Key terms

Primrose League: founded in 1883 as a means of connecting the landed classes in the Conservative Party with the middle and working classes. It organised social activities, often held on the estates of local landowners, but was also active during elections distributing leaflets and persuading voters. By 1900, it had over a million members. The League was also important in involving women from all social classes in politics, though in an auxiliary role.

Tory: another name for Conservatives. 'Tory' like 'Whig' can be traced back to the late-17th century and was originally a term of abuse. From the 1870s, 'Conservative' began to replace 'Tory'. Similarly, 'Liberal' began to replace 'Whig'.

Whig: aristocratic families such as the Russells (Dukes of Bedford) and the Cavendishes (Dukes of Devonshire) played a major role in British politics between the late-17th century and the late-19th century. Their country houses were centres of political activity, especially when parliament was not in session, and with their wealth and large estates they wielded great political influence before the age of mass democracy. Lord Hartington, who helped form the Liberal Unionists, was the son of the 7th Duke of Devonshire.

Key term

Nonconformists: sometimes called dissenters, were British Protestants who did not belong to the Church of England (which was the 'Established' Church). Traditionally, nonconformists supported the Liberals, but in the later years of the 19th century their support for that party had weakened. They were particularly strong in Wales but also influential in the industrial areas.

sections of the middle classes, **nonconformists** (a religious group that did not agree with the beliefs and practices of the Church of England), and radical working men. Under the leadership of William Gladstone, the Liberals had been in government four times between 1868 and 1894 but had suffered badly from the internal divisions over Home Rule.

'Gladstonian' Liberals were mostly agreed on certain broad policies. They were strongly in favour of Free Trade – keeping trade free of tariffs (taxes placed on imports) and quotas, in order to foster competitiveness and efficiency. Another Liberal principle was 'laissez-faire' (literally 'to leave alone') – the belief that the State should intervene as little as possible in society or the economy. Liberals often spoke of the need to keep the role of government limited, having low taxation, and protecting the interests of the nonconformists against the established Church of England. Perhaps, above all, Liberals were reformers, promoting education, defending the rights and freedoms of the individual, and pressuring the ruling classes to lessen the effects of privilege.

After 1886, however, Liberal electoral fortunes declined. For only 3 of the 20 years after 1886 did the Liberals form a government. Gladstone's support for Home Rule for Ireland caused a deep split in the party. Liberal Unionists broke away and drifted into alliance with the Conservatives. Further divisions occurred over the empire. Traditionally, the Liberals were hostile to imperialism but a group of Liberal imperialists led by Lord Rosebery wanted the party to take a more positive attitude towards it. The division became even more bitter during the Boer War of 1899–1902. Again, the Liberals divided between those supporting and those opposing the war.

When the dominating personality of William Gladstone was removed by his resignation as Liberal prime minister in 1894, following the House of Lords' veto of the Home Rule Bill passed by the Commons, the Liberal Party was plunged into a prolonged dispute about the leadership and about the general direction of party policy. Liberal support became narrowly based on the 'Celtic fringe' in Wales, Scotland and Ireland, and on the northern industrial areas of England. The main emphasis of Liberalism in these areas differed. In Wales, a major issue was the disestablishment of the Anglican Church; elsewhere the major concerns were the Boer War, the financing of church schools, or the struggle between the temperance wing of the party and the brewing industry.

The Labour Party

The Labour party was small in 1906 but already a growing political force. Attempts had been made in the 1880s to found a political party to represent the trade unions and working classes. None, however, had succeeded in getting MPs elected. There were a few working-class MPs, mostly trade unionists, but they sat with the Liberals and were often called Lib-Labs. In 1892, Keir Hardie, founder of the Independent Labour Party (ILP), took his seat as the first Labour MP. He lost his seat in 1895 and it was not until 1900 that the modern British Labour Party really began, when representatives from some trade unions, the ILP and various socialist societies formed the Labour Representation Committee (LRC). The LRC managed to gain two seats in the election of 1900 and made a political breakthrough by winning 29 seats in 1906. At that point it changed its name to the Labour Party.

Keir Hardie

Keir Hardie (1856–1915), the 'father' of the modern Labour Party was a self-educated Scottish miner and trade unionist. Originally a Liberal, he aimed to bring socialists and trade unionists together in a separate Labour movement. He was the first elected Labour MP (and insisted on wearing a cloth cap instead of a top hat, to demonstrate his class sympathies). Hardie founded the Independent Labour Party in 1893 and played a central role in the formation of the LRC in 1900. In 1906, he became the first leader of the Labour Party. He did not live long enough to see Labour in government.

The LRC was a group of trade unions and socialist organisations rather than a party. Membership came through **affiliation** and party funds were very limited. In many ways it was more of a **pressure group** than a political party. Its purpose was to form a distinct group in parliament, to promote legislation that would benefit trade unions and manual workers generally. It also aimed to get more working class and trade union **sponsored MPs** into the House of Commons. More specifically, it aimed at legislation to reverse previous legal decisions against the interests and rights of trade unions. Though its leader, Hardie, was committed to building **Socialism** in Britain, not all supporters of the LRC shared the same aims. The Labour Party did grow – from two MPs in 1900 to 42 MPs in the election of December 1910 – but Labour was overshadowed by the Liberals in the years before 1914.

The Irish Nationalist Party

The Irish Nationalist Party (INP) was founded in the 1860s to promote the idea of **Home Rule for Ireland**. Its support came almost entirely from the predominantly Catholic areas of Ireland. As a result of the brilliant leadership of Charles Stewart Parnell, it regularly returned around 80 MPs to Westminster and became a significant force in British politics. In 1885, and again in 1892, the Irish Nationalists held the balance of power at Westminster. Parnell's career, however, ended in 1891 with his disgrace and early death. This divided the party and caused a long leadership struggle. The party's new leader from 1900, John Redmond, never had the same control over his party as Parnell had had. Moreover the Liberals no longer wished to be tied to Irish Home Rule; and the INP had no hope of ever passing Home Rule by themselves. Redmond had to wait for a political situation that might bring support from the main parties for Irish Home Rule. This did not occur until 1911.

■ The political situation from December 1905 to January 1906

In December 1905, the Conservatives were in government but faced mounting criticism and a downturn in trade. The Conservative prime minister, A. J. Balfour, did something unusual. Rather than call a general election, he decided simply to announce his party's resignation from government. As a result, a Liberal government took over and in January 1906 the Liberals, under their leader Campbell-Bannerman, called a general election.

Affiliation: means to link to. Gradually in the 1900s more and more trade unions linked up with the LRC/Labour Party providing members and money.

Pressure group: an organisation of like-minded people who promote a certain cause, and put pressure on parliament or on the government to legislate in favour of that cause. They seek to influence government rather than become the government.

Sponsored MPs: MPs who received support and funding from bodies outside of parliament such as trade unions. Before 1911, MPs did not get a salary from the State and so working-class MPs needed financial support from their trade unions.

Socialism: implies equality and, in its most extreme form, common ownership. The Labour Party's new constitution in 1918 included the famous clause 4 about 'common ownership of the means of production' which sounded far more 'socialist', and therefore frightening to the propertied classes, than it really was.

Home Rule for Ireland: between the Act of Union in 1800 and the Anglo-Irish Treaty of 1921, the whole of Ireland was part of the United Kingdom. Home Rule was the proposal that Ireland should have its own parliament and government whilst remaining within the United Kingdom. Two attempts to pass Home Rule in 1886 and 1893 failed. The first was defeated in the House of Commons the second was vetoed by the Unionist dominated House of Lords.

■ Timeline

The colours represent events relating to Britain during the period: Political, Social, International, Economic

1899–1902	1906	1908	1909	1910	1911	1911–2
Britain's self-confidence jolted by the setbacks of the Boer War	The 'Liberal landslide' in the general election	Start of the social reforms known as the 'New Liberalism'	Rejection of the 'People's Budget' proposed by Lloyd George	Constitutional crisis over the role of the House of Lords	The powers of the Lords cut back by the Parliament Act	Railway, mining and coal strikes

1922	1923	1924	1925	1926	1927
Large cuts in public spending recommended by the 'Geddes Axe'. Lloyd George's coalition replaced by Conservative government under Bonar Law	Bonar Law replaced by Baldwin. Defeat of Conservatives in general election	Minority Labour government under Ramsay MacDonald. Baldwin and the Conservatives return to power after October general election	Britain put back on the Gold Standard	The General Strike	Trade Disputes and Trade Unions Act passed by Conservative government

1937	1938	1939	1940	1941	1942	1943
Replacement of Baldwin by Neville Chamberlain as prime minister	The culmination of Chamberlain's policy of 'Appeasement' at Munich	Declaration of war against Germany. Start of the 'phoney war'	Rapid German victories in the West and British evacuation from Dunkirk. Resignation of Chamberlain. New war coalition formed under Churchill. The Battle of Britain	American support for Britain through 'Lend-Lease'. German invasion of the USSR. Start of true World War with the involvement of the United States and Japan	Humiliating surrender of Singapore. Victories in North Africa. The Beveridge Report issued	Anglo-American invasion of Italy and overthrow of Mussolini

1912–4	1914–5	1916	1917	1918	1919	1920	1921
Ulster crisis caused by Unionist hostility to Irish Home Rule	Outbreak of First World War and formation of coalition government under Asquith	Introduction of conscription. Easter Rising in Dublin. Asquith replaced by Lloyd George.	American entry into the war. The Bolshevik Revolution in Russia	End of the First World War. The 'coupon election'. Votes for women secured by the Representation of the People Act	The Paris peace settlement. Start of the Anglo-Irish War	Formation of the Communist Party of Great Britain	Miners' strike. Treaty with Irish Nationalists. Proclamation of Irish Free State

1928	1929	1931	1932	1933	1935	1936
Equal voting rights for women secured by Suffrage Act	May general election and formation of Ramsay MacDonald's second Labour government. Wall Street crash	Financial crisis. Collapse of the Labour government. Formation of the National government under MacDonald. The Gold Standard abandoned. Labour reduced to 52 seats after general election	Protective tariffs introduced. Formation of Mosley's British Union of Fascists	Establishment of Adolf Hitler's Nazi regime in Germany	General election and confirmation of Conservative domination of the National government. Resignation of Ramsay MacDonald and return of Baldwin as prime minister	The Abdication Crisis. The Public Order Act passed to restrict political extremism

1944	1945	1947	1948	1949	1950	1951
D-Day landings and liberation of occupied Europe. Butler's Education Act passed	End of Second World War. Majority Labour government formed under Attlee after 'Labour landslide'	'Austerity' policies after severe winter and financial crisis. British withdrawal from India. Nationalisation of the coal industry. Launch of the Marshall Plan	Establishment of the National Health Service	Formation of NATO. Devaluation of the pound	Start of the Korean War. Labour re-elected with reduced majority	Festival of Britain. Labour defeated in general election. Start of 13 years of Conservative governments

1 The 'Liberal landslide', 1906

In this chapter you will learn about:

- the reasons for the Liberal landslide victory in the 1906 general election

- the impact on Britain of the 1906 election result

- the position of the emerging Labour Party in 1906.

Fig. 1 *Henry Campbell-Bannerman – 'C-B' – Scottish-born British statesman. Liberal prime minister 1905–8*

Key term

Landslide: a landslide election victory is one in which one party wins a huge majority of seats over all other parties in the House of Commons, reversing the previous government majority. Such 'landslides' also happened for Labour in 1945 and for 'New Labour' in 1997.

I wonder what Parliament House will be,
In nineteen hundred and six,
We know that 'C-B' the premier will be
In nineteen hundred and six.

1 *Extract from 'Liberal election song' composed by S. E. Boyle*

Key profile

Henry Campbell-Bannerman

Henry Campbell-Bannerman (1836–1908), often referred to as 'C-B', was leader of the Liberal Party from 1898 to 1908 and Liberal prime minister from 1905 to 1908. He managed to reunite the Liberal Party and shrewdly called a general election early in 1906 winning with a huge majority. Illness forced him to retire in 1908.

The general election called in January 1906 produced one of the decisive election results of the 20th century. It was a **landslide** victory for the Liberal Party. Not only did the Liberals win a majority in the House of Commons, they won a huge overall majority with around 400 seats as against 157 for the Conservatives. Most of the Conservative cabinet lost their seats, including the prime minister A. J. Balfour. It was to be 1922 before the Conservatives won an election again. Across Britain the 'swing' to the Liberals was about 10 per cent. The steady drift towards the Conservatives in Lancashire, the heart of Britain's manufacturing district, which had been evident since 1868, was thrown into reverse. The Liberals also made notable gains in London and the south east. Birmingham was a lone exception, remaining loyal to the Conservatives because of the strength of local support for Joseph Chamberlain, and because of the effectiveness of his formidable local political 'machine'. The scale of this Liberal victory was especially surprising because the Liberals had not been in government for 20 years except briefly in 1892–5. In the 1900 election, they had been soundly beaten. Now, in 1906, they were overwhelmingly victorious. The 1906 election also had wider results including the emergence of the Labour Party as a distinct force in the House of Commons.

Table 1 *General election results for British political parties, 1892–1906*

Date	Conservative		Liberal		Labour	
	No. of seats	% vote	No. of seats	% vote	No. of seats	% vote
1892	314	47	272	45		
1895	411	49	177	45.7		
1900	402	51.5	184	44.6	2	1.8
1906	157	43.6	401	49	29	6

Activity

Statistical analysis

With reference to the election statistics 1892–1906 in Table 1:

1. Comment on how the different political parties had performed in the years before 1906.

2. What was the scale of the Conservative defeat in 1906?

3. In what ways was the 1906 election 'an amazing victory' for the Liberals?

4. Comment on the Labour Party result.

Cross-reference

Joseph Chamberlain is profiled later in this chapter on page 10.

The general election, 1906

Fig. 2 *Joyful scene at the National Liberal Club, after the announcement of the defeat of the Conservative leader, Balfour, in his Manchester constituency, 20 January 1906*

Activity

Thinking point

The 1906 general election has encouraged debate about whether the result was due primarily to Conservative weaknesses or to Liberal strengths. Construct a chart summarising Conservative failings and Liberal strengths between 1902 and 1906, and reach your own conclusion.

Factors weakening the Conservatives before 1906

All general election results can be assessed in terms of whether the factors causing one side to win are more or less important than the factors causing the other side to lose. In the decade before 1906, the Conservatives had won two general elections with large overall majorities, whilst the Liberals appeared divided and demoralised. Yet, in 1906, the Conservatives experienced their greatest electoral defeat and the Liberals

■ Exploring the detail

The Boer War

The Boer War (1899–1902) took place in South Africa. The Boers were farmers of Dutch descent living in the Transvaal and Orange Free State. The discovery of gold and diamonds in the Transvaal had led to an influx of British miners ('Uitlanders') and tensions between the groups led to war. Despite the ultimate British victory, which was prematurely exploited by the Conservatives in the 1900 'khaki' election, the scandal of the British 'concentration camps' to intern non-combatant Boers, concerns about the malnutrition of army volunteers and the length of the war raised important political questions.

■ Cross-reference

The issue of **Free Trade** and Chamberlain's **tariff reform** campaign is discussed on pages 12 and 13.

their greatest electoral triumph. There were many reasons for this stunning reversal of political fortunes, not only in the leadership of the two main parties and the campaigns they fought, but also in the impact of recent events and political developments.

The Boer War

One of these key events was the Boer War. In the short term, the Boer War benefited the Conservatives; in the longer term it contributed to their defeat in 1906. In 1900, the Boer War had helped the Conservatives to win an impressive electoral victory. This was partly because of patriotic support for the government but also because the war split the Liberal Party. However, in the longer run, the Boer War sowed some of the seeds of the Conservatives' great defeat in 1906. The war was far more costly in lives and money than had been expected and some of the methods used to defeat the Boers caused moral outrage in Britain.

The Boer War also revealed the effect of poverty in the cities and the need for social reforms. The Liberals gained support by claiming that the Conservatives had neglected this. The war also had the effect of encouraging Joseph Chamberlain to push his campaign for tariff reform – this issue divided the party in the Conservative electoral campaign in 1906. Furthermore, the end of the war in 1902 gave the Liberals the opportunity to heal their divisions and offer a real alternative to the Conservatives.

■ Key profile

Joseph Chamberlain

Joseph Chamberlain (1836–1914) was the man who split two parties. He was a leading figure on the radical wing of the Liberal Party until he broke away in 1886 because he opposed Home Rule for Ireland. He was then a leading figure in the Liberal Unionists allied with the Conservative Party until he resigned from Balfour's government to campaign for protective tariffs and imperial preference.

The 1902 Education Act

The Conservatives' Education Act of 1902 roused the fury of the nonconformists and led many of them to revert to the Liberal Party. Before 1902, Anglican and Catholic schools had been funded by their churches; the 1902 Act provided for all schools to be funded from **local rates**. Nonconformists were outraged that their taxes might be spent on schools to which they strongly objected.

A great campaign was launched against the act. Some English nonconformists refused to pay their taxes while in Wales an orchestrated campaign was whipped up by the Liberal MP David Lloyd George. He addressed a conference in Cardiff in 1903 and suggested that the Welsh refuse rate aid to Anglican schools, on the grounds that they were in poor repair – an excuse which just made the campaign legal. He also successfully persuaded them to show their disapproval of this Conservative policy by electing Liberals in the Welsh 1904 county council elections.

■ Key term

Local rates: local taxes levied by the local authority to pay for local services.

■ Cross-reference

For more information on **David Lloyd George**, look ahead to page 17.

The 1904 Licensing Act

The Licensing Act of 1904 was another issue that annoyed nonconformist voters. The act aimed at reducing the number of public houses, but it infuriated the temperance section of the nonconformists by proposing to compensate brewers and publicans for the cancellation of licences. Since the brewers were supporters of the Conservatives, nonconformists denounced the 1904 Act as a 'brewers' bill'. Most nonconformists had traditionally voted Liberal rather than Conservative anyway, but many had switched away from the Liberals over Home Rule for Ireland. Now they returned to voting Liberal. Moreover, nonconformists were strong in areas like Wales and could help swing the vote in marginal **constituencies**.

Evidence from **by-elections** suggests Liberal support increased after the disagreements over the 1902 and 1904 Acts. The intense nonconformist opposition to the Education and Licensing Acts also seems to have encouraged a revival of the Liberal Party after its divisions over the Boer War. The campaigns helped reunite the Liberals and so laid the basis for success in 1906. Even so, this cannot alone explain the scale of the Conservative defeat in 1906.

The Chinese labour issue

The so-called 'Chinese slavery' issue between 1902 and 1904 caused a scandal that damaged the Conservative government in the eyes not only of nonconformists but of another social group – **trade unionists**. Chinese labourers, who would work for very low wages, were being imported into South Africa. Not only did this raise a moral outcry by nonconformists about the treatment of the Chinese, but British trade unions feared that employers might bring them into Britain, so pushing down wages at home. With unemployment high in 1905 and with inadequate support for the unemployed, opposition to 'Chinese slavery' took votes away from the Conservatives.

The Taff Vale case

The Conservatives lost support because of their failure to take the part of the trade unions over the Taff Vale case. In 1901, a dispute had broken out in Wales between the Taff Vale Railway Company and the railway workers' trade union, which had led to strike action. The company took the trade union to court, demanding compensation for loss of profits during the strike. In 1902, the House of Lords, the highest court in the land, ruled that a company was within its rights to sue a trade union. The trade unions were horrified, as this made it almost impossible for them to call successful strikes. Only an Act of Parliament could over-rule a Lords' judgement and the Conservatives refused to introduce such legislation. This encouraged trade union support for the idea of a Labour group in parliament and for campaigning against the Conservatives in the election.

Neglect of social reform

Although the 1906 election was not fought on the issue of social reform, there was a growing awareness of the extent of poverty in Britain in the early 1900s. The Boer War had exposed the amount of malnutrition especially in the cities and led to concerns about the physical decline of the British race. Some Liberals were already working out a new form of Liberalism in which the State would play a greater role in ensuring minimum living standards for the most vulnerable, and the new LRC was also campaigning for sweeping reforms. Despite all this, the

Key terms

Constituencies: a parliamentary constituency is an area of the country that elects a member of parliament to represent it in the House of Commons. In 1906, the United Kingdom had over 600 constituencies.

By-elections: a by-election occurs between general elections (which are held at a maximum every five years) when a serving MP dies or resigns from his position. An election is held within that MP's constituency to elect a new MP to replace him. By-elections are sometimes thought to reflect the public's opinion of the serving government – supporting it, by electing its representative, or showing displeasure, by turning to a different party.

Trade unions: also known as 'organised labour', trade unions formed in the 19th century and grew rapidly in the 20th century. They enabled workers to negotiate collectively with their employers about wages and conditions. Workers not in trade unions, that is, unorganised, were less able to negotiate effectively with their employers.

Cross-reference

The concepts of **'New Liberalism'** are covered on page 16.

To recap on the **Labour Representation Committee**, see page 4.

Conservatives produced nothing other than Balfour's 1902 Education Act. Although this did provide for reform – not only in terms of school funding, by allowing for financial support from local rates, but also by making local authorities responsible for organising secondary and higher education – it proved highly controversial and actually benefited the Liberals (by stirring up opposition) more than the Conservatives.

The tariff reform campaign

Tariff reform was probably the Conservatives' biggest policy misjudgement. In 1903, the tariff reform campaign was launched in Birmingham by Joseph Chamberlain. He wanted to reintroduce tariffs, with a lower level tariff for goods coming into Britain from the empire than for goods imported from non-empire countries. This policy was known as Imperial Protectionism. Chamberlain argued that this would protect British jobs, help pay for social reforms and strengthen Britain's position in the world by integrating the empire into an effective unit.

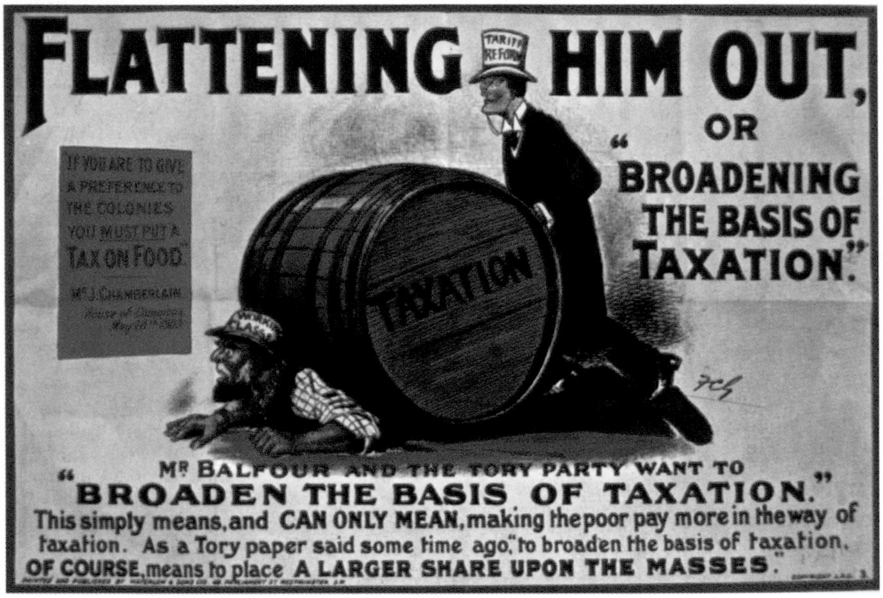

However, tariff reform damaged the Conservatives. Many voters, both working and middle class, feared that tariffs would mean dearer food and falling living standards. Tariff reform divided the Conservative government and party. One leading Conservative, Winston Churchill, actually voted with the Liberals on this issue in 1904. On the other hand, this issue helped to reunite and strengthen the Liberal Party because belief in Free Trade was something all Liberals strongly supported.

Fig. 3 *Liberal poster in 1906 election, showing Joseph Chamberlain, the Tory Protectionist crushing the workers with his high tariffs on imported foods and goods*

The Conservative leadership

A. J. Balfour's position as Conservative prime minister after Salisbury's death in 1902 did not help the Conservative cause. Although highly intelligent, Balfour lacked political skill. He was not as sensitive to public opinion as Salisbury, proved indecisive on tariffs and seriously miscalculated the reaction of the working classes on key issues. Balfour had piloted the 1902 Education Bill through parliament and so incurred the hostility of the nonconformists. He failed to foresee the anger that both the Chinese labour issue and his refusal to reverse Taff Vale would cause amongst British working men. Balfour misunderstood working men's reaction to the tariff reform campaign and he allowed Joseph Chamberlain to make tariff reform a key Unionist policy from 1903 onwards. Furthermore, he was indirectly responsible for the timing of the 1906 election through his unusual decision that his government should step down in December 1905.

■ **Cross-reference**

Winston Churchill is profiled on page 17, and his later prominence is discussed in detail on page 98.

■ **Cross-reference**

The events of **December 1905** are described on page 5.

■ Key profile

A. J. Balfour

Arthur J. Balfour (1848–1930) was the nephew of Lord Salisbury. He acted as leader of the Commons during his uncle's premiership and succeeded him as Conservative prime minister in 1902 (hence the phrase 'Bob's y'er uncle'). He was a solitary, intellectual figure and a poor speaker. His miscalculations contributed to the great Conservative election defeat of 1906 and he led his party unsuccessfully through the two general elections of 1910. He resigned as leader in 1911 after a 'Balfour must go' campaign from his own backbenchers, but he remained in politics until 1929.

Fig. 4 *Arthur James Balfour – Scottish-born Conservative statesman and prime minister 1902–5*

Attractions of the Liberal Party

By 1905, the Liberals were also a reunited party. Issues that had divided them, such as Irish Home Rule, were put to one side, the Boer War was over and agreement had been reached about the leadership of the party. Moreover, all Liberals were united behind the banner of Free Trade. During the election campaign in 1906, the Liberals exploited this commitment to great effect. Free Trade was literally a '**bread and butter**' issue of great concern to voters in all classes. Henry Campbell-Bannerman promoted a 'broad' party that was not dominated by any one issue (except perhaps Free Trade), nor by any one group.

The Liberals were able to exploit Conservative mistakes in regard to the trade unions and could also win nonconformist support by exploiting the Conservative misjudgements over education and licensing, as well as by promising Welsh **Disestablishment**. Irish voters in Britain were more likely to vote Liberal with its support for Home Rule than the anti-Home Rule Unionists.

The Lib-Lab Pact

■ Key terms

'Bread and butter' issue: one that affects people's everyday life. In this case, the Free Trade question was directly linked to the cost of food on people's tables.

Disestablishment: this would have led to the removal of the power of the Anglican Church, which was the Established Church in England and Wales and was headed by the monarch. The nonconformists supported this policy, which would have removed the church's control over land and property.

■ Cross-reference

The issues surrounding **Home Rule for Ireland** are outlined on page 5.

Fig. 5 *The parliamentary Labour Party, 1906. Second from left is James Ramsay MacDonald (1866–1937) who later became the first British Labour prime minister. In the centre is Keir Hardie (1856–1915), the 'father' of the Labour Party*

Fig. 6 *Liberal gains in Tory and Nationalist Liverpool. Round the polling-stations and committee-rooms, 20 January 1906*

In 1903, the Liberals forged an agreement with the leader of the LRC, Ramsay MacDonald, whereby the Liberals would not oppose Labour candidates in the next general election in 30 selected constituencies in England and Wales where a Labour candidate was more likely to be able to defeat the Conservatives. In return, the LRC promised to restrict their candidates in other constituencies and so prevent a split in the anti-Conservative vote. This had happened in the north-east Lanark by-election in 1901 and the Liberals wanted to ensure there was no repetition of this which might harm their election chances. Given the rising tide of Liberal support however, this could hardly have been their sole motive. Labour, as a political movement, was far too small to pose a real challenge to the Liberals, so there must have been other factors behind the decision to pool forces. One of these may have been financial. Labour had an election fund of £150,000 and since the pact would remove the need to fight Labour as a rival, it would reduce the Liberals' own election costs. The two parties were also in broad agreement about social reform and working-class reform. The Liberal/Labour joint campaigns against the 1902 Education Act and 'Chinese slavery' helped reinforce this.

Both Liberals and Labour also shared similar ideas with regard to Free Trade, which not only promised cheap food but was also bound up with the idea of peace and 'international harmony', causes dear to the hearts of both groups. MacDonald was a moderate leader and radical socialist ideas seemed to be confined to the more extreme fringes of the movement, so Labour seemed safe allies. The Liberal Party was convinced they stood to gain more than they would lose through this alliance.

The LRC spent the ensuing years getting organised, establishing constituency branches and drawing up a manifesto. Eventually, the LRC put up 50 candidates in the 1906 election and managed to win 29 seats, just five of which had been gained against Liberal opposition. (This was increased to 30 shortly after the election when a Durham miner MP chose to join Labour.) The pact had obviously worked well for the embryonic party, giving the LRC new political power that led to their adoption of the title 'The Labour Party'. It increased the size of the Conservative defeat, but whether the Liberals had really done themselves a service is another question.

Summary of the key issues

Between 1902 and 1905, the Conservative leadership managed to alienate important sections of the voting public and drive them away from the Unionist Party. In doing so, they also helped revive and strengthen the Liberals. The Liberals had more to offer the voters than they had in 1900. Nevertheless, their campaign was essentially negative rather than positive. Little was made of social reform; rather the Liberals focused on the failings of the previous Conservative government and so were able to enjoy a wide appeal across the political and social spectrum. The question was whether they would be able to maintain that wide appeal without a more positive programme, especially given the rise of Labour as a new, radical party on the left. With hindsight, the Liberal victory of 1906 seems ambivalent. On the one hand, it was to usher in the greatest period of Liberal government in the 20th century; on the other hand, it was to be the last time the Liberals ever won an election outright.

Summary questions

1 Explain why the electoral chances of the Liberal Party improved between 1900 and 1906.

2 How important was Chamberlain's tariff reform campaign to the outcome of the 1906 election?

The 'New Liberalism'

The Land! The Land! 'Twas God that made the Land:
The Land! The Land! The ground on which we stand.
Why should we beggars be with the ballot in our hand?
God gave the Land for the People.

1

Song of the Budget League, sung to the tune of 'Marching through Georgia'

Even before 1906, individuals within the broader Liberal movement were already looking for a new direction in Liberalism. This search for new policies was partly due to the divisions within the party after Gladstone's retirement in 1894, and partly a reaction to the electoral defeats in 1895 and 1900, but it was also influenced by the growing awareness of the extent of poverty and the need to do something about it. Intellectuals such as T. H. Green, L. T. Hobhouse and J. A. Hobson recognised that 19th century Liberalism had put too much stress on the freedom of the individual and not enough on the role of society through the State. There was also a practical political motive – many Liberals were worried about the stirring of the Labour movement as a potential political rival.

Between 1906 and 1914, the new Liberal government carried through a programme of major social reforms. It is sometimes claimed that these reforms laid the foundations for a 'welfare state' in Britain.

The growth of New Liberalism

Cross-reference

Liberalism and its key beliefs before 1906 are discussed on pages 3–4.

'New Liberalism' was the name given to the reformist ideology of elements in the Liberal Party. Whereas 19th century or 'classical' Liberalism had stressed freedom to *do* things – such as freedom to worship, to publish, or to criticise government – New Liberalism stressed in addition, freedom *from* evils such as poverty, low wages and insecurity. Classical Liberalism had promoted laissez-faire but New Liberalism believed that intervention by the State had a key role in establishing minimum standards of life. Whereas Old Liberalism stressed 'self-help', New Liberalism recognised that the poorer sections of society needed some help from the State as well. New Liberalism put greater emphasis on the State's role in providing 'safety-nets' to prevent hard-working but vulnerable citizens falling into destitution.

Nevertheless, New Liberalism was not a belief that suggested everyone should receive State assistance; it only stressed the need to help those who were vulnerable and unable to help themselves. There was also a lot of continuity between 'Old' and 'New' Liberalism – the ideal of 'self-help' was present in both. New Liberals believed the State should continue to leave those who were able to look after themselves to do so and they continued to believe in Free Trade and in freedom to do business without control.

However, New Liberalism implied higher government spending which contradicted the traditional Liberal emphasis on thrift and low taxation. Some supporters believed in a scheme of contributory payments in return for benefits for certain groups, as had been pioneered in Germany and New Zealand. Other, more radical Liberals believed there should be some element of redistribution of income by taxing the rich more heavily and diverting some of the money to the poor.

The Liberals had not won the 1906 election on a 'New Liberal' platform, however. The election had been fought on a variety of issues, principally Free Trade versus tariff reform. Nevertheless, from 1906, and especially from 1908 onwards, the Liberal governments of H. Campbell-Bannerman and H. H. Asquith were to pass a series of social and welfare reforms. A policy of social reform had useful political advantages. Social reform was an area in which the Conservatives were vulnerable to attack. Bringing in such reforms could defuse the potential threat from the newly-formed Labour Party. It could also rescue the Liberal Party from its recent divisions over issues such as Home Rule for Ireland and give the party a theme that might unite it.

Two 'New Liberal' ministers in particular, David Lloyd George and Winston S. Churchill, were to be associated with the greatest of these reforms.

Key profiles

H. H. Asquith

H. H. Asquith (1852–1928) succeeded Campbell-Bannerman as Liberal prime minister in 1908. He presided over the great Liberal social and political reforms between 1908 and 1914 and dealt quite effectively with a variety of new challenges. However, during the Great War it was felt that he was not pushing through vigorously enough the changes Britain needed to make. As a result, he was replaced as prime minister by David Lloyd George early in 1916. He never forgave Lloyd George and the vendetta between the two men helped split and weaken the Liberal Party from 1916 until Asquith's death in 1928.

David Lloyd George

Brought up in north Wales by his shoemaker uncle, David Lloyd George became a local solicitor and in 1890 Liberal MP for Caernafon Boroughs. He first became prominent for his opposition to the Boer War. Labelled a 'pro-Boer' he was lucky to escape alive when a 30,000-strong mob stormed Birmingham Town Hall where he was giving a speech. His quick mind, skill as a public speaker and ability to get things done led to his appointment as president of the Board of Trade in the Liberal government of 1906 and then Chancellor of the Exchequer in 1908.

Winston Churchill

Winston Churchill, grandson of the Duke of Marlborough, was first a soldier, then a war correspondent before entering parliament as MP for Oldham in 1900. Originally an unconventional Conservative, he became a Liberal in 1904. Churchill followed his friend, Lloyd George, as president of the Board of Trade 1908–10. In this post Churchill cooperated with Lloyd George in putting through major social reforms. In 1910, Churchill was appointed Home Secretary and First Lord of the Admiralty in 1911. Later he would become a Conservative MP, Chancellor of the Exchequer in 1925 and prime minister 1940–5 and 1951–5.

Cross-reference

To recap on **Sir Henry Campbell-Bannermann** see page 8.

Fig. 1 *Herbert Henry Asquith – Liberal statesman. Prime minister 1908–16*

Fig. 2 *An uncharacteristically restrained David Lloyd George as a young but ambitious minister in the Liberal government of 1906*

The problem of poverty

Fig. 3 *Female inmates of an Edwardian workhouse. By the 1900s, most workhouses were no longer as grim as those portrayed in Dickens 50 years earlier, but the term 'workhouse' could still produce anxiety in the minds of the elderly*

■ **Cross-reference**

The spread of **trade unionism** is covered on page 11.

■ **Exploring the detail**

Help for the poor in the early 20th century

There was virtually no State provision for the poor at the start of the century because of the prevailing belief in laissez-faire. The poor were therefore left to beg or turn to private charities. Many, such as Dr Barnardos, set up in 1867, were concerned with orphan children, but far fewer offered help to the elderly. For them, the Poor Law remained the last resort, offering either 'outdoor relief' paid to the needy in their own homes, or the parish workhouse. Beyond this, there were some who earned just enough to afford some private insurance – perhaps through their trade union or working men's club – but the provision was often inadequate and prolonged periods of unemployment meant that many policies lapsed.

In the later 19th century there had been growing concern about the extent of poverty. The population of Britain more than trebled in the 19th century and so there were larger numbers of the poor than ever before. The population was increasingly urbanised, which concentrated poverty in the 'slum' districts of every town and city. For those who chose to look, and an increasing number of philanthropists, charitable societies, writers and researchers did choose to do so, the problem of poverty was visible and acute. It also highlighted the contrast between the sometimes appalling poverty of the slums and the openly displayed riches of the wealthy. Fears of disorder and revolution, particularly after the development of 'new' trade unions of unskilled workers brought a wave of strikes in the later 19th century, helped to create a climate that was favourable to measures that might alleviate poverty and the problems arising from unemployment.

The most important research findings to influence public opinion were the social surveys of Charles Booth and Seebohm Rowntree. Booth published 17 volumes on the life and labour of London's poor between 1889 and 1903, while Rowntree, setting out to test Booth's statistics in York, began his investigation in 1899. Their conclusions were startling and worrying. Both Booth and Rowntree estimated that up to 30 per cent of the urban population could be classified as 'poor' and that about 10 per cent might be classified as 'very poor', or as living in 'primary poverty'. This bottom 10 per cent had insufficient income to meet the bare minimum standard of living. Another 20 per cent had incomes only just sufficient to meet the minimum standard. Although Booth and Rowntree studied towns in their earliest studies, later ones showed a similar result in rural areas. This meant that in the richest country in the world more than a quarter of the population lived just at or even below subsistence level, the bare minimum on which a person could be expected to live.

Booth and Rowntree also showed that even those who could just meet the bare necessities of life could fall into abject poverty through factors beyond their control. They pointed out that it was not just the weaknesses of individuals, such as idleness or wastefulness that caused poverty, but factors beyond the control of even the most hard-working and careful individual. These included the economic forces that led to unemployment, irregular work and low wages and the unavoidable factors such as old age, sickness and the premature death of the main wage earner. Families were also affected by lack of education and decent housing. Clearly, the answer to these problems required an approach by society as a whole, rather than leaving things entirely to the individual.

The development of New Liberalism was also complemented by the campaign for national efficiency which had arisen at the end of the Boer War. This was based on a commonly-held belief that Britain needed reform if it was going to maintain its status as a great power. The war had revealed that a high percentage of young men were medically unfit for military service, and as a result there were worries about the physical deterioration of the British race. This also coincided with Britain being overtaken economically by Germany and the USA as an industrial nation. The national efficiency movement therefore campaigned, among other things, for better diet and medical care for the next generation. The belief in the need for reform, although wider in its concerns than just social reform, encouraged greater State involvement in areas such as education and child welfare.

The influence of New Liberalism on the Liberal government from 1906

Between 1906 and 1908, the ideas of New Liberalism seem to have had relatively little influence on the new government. Although there were measures of social reform, particularly concerned with children, these were a response to the movement for national efficiency and pressure from Labour MPs and do not seem to have been directly inspired by the ideas of New Liberalism. The prime minister, Campbell-Bannerman, remained essentially a traditional Liberal, and most of the measures passed during his time in office concerned the issues on which the Liberals had campaigned against the Conservatives in 1906 or fulfilled promises made to their Labour allies. The importing of Chinese labour into South Africa was ended, a Trade Disputes Act was passed in 1906 to reverse the Taff Vale judgement, a new education bill was introduced to satisfy the nonconformists (although it was defeated in the House of Lords), and an improvement was made in regard to workmen's compensation.

After the resignation of Campbell-Bannerman in 1908, the pace of social reform accelerated and the reforms became more radical. Most of the post-1908 reforms were the work of David Lloyd George and Winston Churchill. Opinion is divided, however, as to when Lloyd George can be said to have converted to New Liberalism. Some of his speeches during the 1906 election show a desire for the Liberals to tackle social problems, though more in order to prevent the growth of a rival Labour Party than because of New Liberal philosophy. Other speeches refer to old age pensions but these seem to have been designed to attack Joseph Chamberlain for not delivering them, rather than advocating any detailed plan of Lloyd George's own. In 1908, Lloyd George went to Germany to study the practical details of their system of social insurance started in the 1880s, and this may have inspired him. However, it is unlikely he would have gone on this visit had he not already been thinking of carrying out something similar in Britain.

Exploring the detail

Charles Booth and Seebohm Rowntree

Charles Booth came from a wealthy Liverpool family but decided to make a detailed study of London's poor. He produced the most detailed survey of poverty ever attempted and showed the social conditions of every street with colour coding as to the degree of poverty/wealth.

Seebohm Rowntree was the son of a successful chocolate manufacturer and recorded his observations of York in *Poverty, A Study of Town Life* published in 1901. Rowntree became a close friend of Lloyd George and continued to make studies of poverty, for example on rural conditions (published 1913) and York (1941) and (1951).

Activity

Revision exercise

Make a spider diagram to illustrate the various factors that helped create a climate favourable to social welfare reform in the early 20th century.

Cross-reference

To review issues such as **Chinese labour**, **Taff Vale**, and the dissatisfaction of the **nonconformists**, see page 11.

■ Liberal social reforms

Between 1906 and 1914, the Liberal government introduced a series of social reforms to address the problems of poverty. These were effective to varying degrees.

Table 1 *Effectiveness of Liberal social reforms*

Date	Title	Details	Strengths	Limitations
1906	Education Act (provision of meals)	Local authorities given power to provide free school meals for needy children.	Enabled hungry children to concentrate more and so learn more effectively. By 1914, a total of 14 million free school meals a year were being provided by LEAs.	Permissive, not compulsory. Not all LEAs used this power before 1914. Even in 1913 only about half LEAs were providing free meals.
1907	Education Act (medical inspection)	Set up the School Medical Service and made it compulsory for LEAs to medically inspect school children.	By 1914, three-quarters of LEAs were providing free medical inspection and two-thirds some form of free medical treatment.	Provided only a very cursory check and not always treatment. Poor not always able to afford to treat the conditions revealed by the inspection.
1908	Children Act and other protective legislation	Made parental neglect illegal. Set up juvenile courts and borstals for young offenders. Made it illegal to sell tobacco and alcohol to children.	State tried to ensure minimum standards of care and protection for children. Differentiating in its treatment of child and adult offenders.	Some new legislation but also a lot of codifying of existing law.
1908	Old Age Pensions Act	Provided a pension of five shillings a week for single persons and 7s and 6d for a married couple.	Scheme was 'non-contributory' being paid out of general taxation not by contributions from the recipients. Provided a regular weekly sum as of right to those who qualified. Paid by the State through local post offices NOT through the Poor Law. This enabled those too ashamed of being classed as 'a pauper' to get help. There were about 1 million pensioners by 1915 with more women than men qualifying.	Only paid to the elderly poor, i.e. those over 70 on a very low income. Pension was based on a 'sliding scale' according to income so only the poorest got the full amount. Pensioners also had to be 'of good character', i.e. have worked regularly and not been in prison. Pension paid was bare minimum for survival. It was only a support not a replacement for self-help.
1909	Trade boards	Boards set up to fix minimum wages and inspect conditions in certain trades.	Initially covered 200,000, mostly women workers in four trades, e.g. tailoring and lace-making, where the hours were long, wages low and there was no trade union to protect the workers. By 1913, this had been extended to six trades and to coal miners too.	Only covered the 'sweated trades', left out many other low paid workers, e.g. in farming. Too few inspectors to enforce rigorously. No national minimum wage until 1999.
	Labour exchanges	Set up places where workers looking for a job and employers looking for workers could meet.	2 million workers had registered by 1914 and the 430 exchanges were finding 3,000 jobs a day.	Has been estimated that for every worker who found a job, three did not. Also the State was not creating jobs for the unemployed, only helping the job market operate more smoothly.

Date	Title	Details	Strengths	Limitations
1911	National Insurance (Unemployment) Act	State compelled workers and their employers, in certain trades, to contribute weekly to a national insurance fund. State topped this up out of taxation. The fund enabled contributing workers to receive a weekly benefit if unemployed.	Covered 2.25 million workers and provided a seven shillings a week benefit for up to 15 weeks. This guaranteed, regular sum enabled families of the unemployed to avoid destitution whilst the breadwinner found another job.	Only applied to certain trades – the 'insured trades'. These were trades known for regular seasonal or cyclical unemployment, e.g. the building and shipbuilding trades. Most workers were not covered by the scheme and had to rely on their own savings, trade unions or private insurance. Only became fully operational in 1912.
	National Insurance (Sickness) Act	State organised compulsory scheme by which workers and their employers paid weekly into a national fund. State topped this up out of general taxation.	Covered some 13 million workers. The scheme paid out a weekly sickness benefit of 10 shillings a week for 13 weeks and then 5 shillings for a further 13 weeks, i.e. 26 weeks or 6 months in total. There was a maternity grant for women workers, a disability benefit and free medical treatment with an approved doctor. There was also free treatment in a sanatorium for those with TB.	Only covered workers earning below £160 pa, everyone else still had to look after themselves. Only covered workers aged 16 to 60 and since OAPs began at 70 there was a 10-year gap in provision. The act also only covered the contributor – usually the father – not his family. Any hospital treatment had to be paid for bar the sanatorium. Only became effective in 1913. In total, only c13 million of the c45 million population were included in the National Insurance Scheme.
1906–11	Other protective legislation	Workmen's Compensation Act, 1906	Extended provisions for compensating workers for work-based accidents and diseases resulting from their occupations.	Not always easy to prove that injuries to health were due to work. Only covered workers earning less than £250 pa.
		Merchant Shipping Act	Improved food and accommodation for merchant seamen.	Only covered British ships and not easy to enforce.
		Shops Act, 1911	Provided weekly half-day holiday for shop workers.	Employers could make up with longer hours on other days.
		Coal Mines Acts, 1908 and 1911	Fixed length of working day underground to eight hours. Improved safety regulations.	Still occupation with long hours and low pay. Did not cover time taken to get to work. Mining remained a dangerous job.

How extensive were the Liberal social reforms?

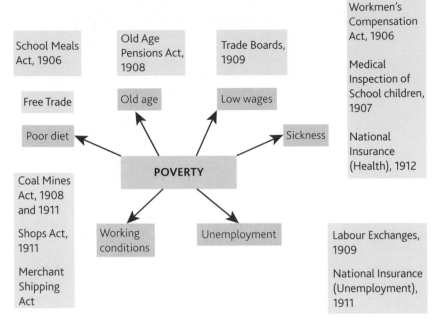

School Meals Act, 1906

Old Age Pensions Act, 1908

Trade Boards, 1909

Workmen's Compensation Act, 1906

Medical Inspection of School children, 1907

National Insurance (Health), 1912

Free Trade

Old age

Low wages

Poor diet

Sickness

POVERTY

Coal Mines Act, 1908 and 1911

Shops Act, 1911

Merchant Shipping Act

Working conditions

Unemployment

Labour Exchanges, 1909

National Insurance (Unemployment), 1911

Fig. 4 *Liberal social reforms, 1906–14*

Activity

Challenge your thinking

Using the list of Liberal reforms given in Table 1, indicate which measures or terms you feel reflected 19th century attitudes (e.g. self-help; distinction between deserving/undeserving poor) and which were genuinely 'new' in their proposals. Explain your views.

Key term

Permissive: the provision of school meals was only a 'permissive' act, as was the Town Planning Act of 1909. Local authorities could choose to carry out these acts or to ignore them, as they wished.

The Liberals never created a full 'welfare state', but it is perhaps unfair to blame them for this, when it had never been their intention anyway. The Liberals did as they intended, and created a basic minimum – or 'a lifebelt', as Churchill described their reforms. However, this meant that major areas were left untouched. Housing, for example, remained in short supply and despite some limited slum clearance under the 1909 Town Planning Act, fighting the entrenched interests of wealthy landlords proved too much of a challenge and the act was left '**permissive**'. Lloyd George certainly had ideas about the provision of local authority or 'council' housing and had planned a major housing act for 1915, but this had to wait until after the Great War.

Fig. 5 *Deprived children enjoy a school dinner courtesy of the local education authority, Camberwell, London, 1910*

The Liberals can be criticised for not attempting to reform the Poor Law, despite the findings of the Royal Commission on the Poor Laws whose investigations, between 1905 and 1909, filled 47 volumes. The commisssion had been first set up by the Conservatives. Although disagreements about the way forward led to the production of separate majority and minority reports, both accepted the need for reform. The majority report favoured a scheme of Public Assistance Committees. The minority report was more radical and advocated a government Ministry of Labour. The Liberals did respond to some of the suggestions by setting up Labour Exchanges providing unemployment insurance, but they never scrapped the old Poor Law and many of the elderly poor had to rely on the workhouse, even after pensions were introduced.

Education was another neglected area. After their 1906 Education Bill, designed to change the Conservatives' 1902 Act, was destroyed by the Lords, the cause was given up. Consequently, the British education system remained inferior to that of its rival, Germany, where the amount spent on technical and higher education was far greater. Despite the 1902 Act, not all local authorities built sufficient secondary schools and most children left school at 13.

There were also other causes of poverty identified in the Booth and Rowntree reports that were left untouched. Despite the provision of some compulsory insurance, the plight of those in casual employment, particularly in the docks, remained dire. Similarly, those with large families received no specific aid. Rowntree undertook a 'follow-up' survey in 1936, which showed that only 4 per cent were living in 'primary poverty', compared with the 10 per cent noted in his first report at the turn of the century. Since by 1936 there had been a war and the survey was made at a time of the Depression, it suggests the reforms set in motion by the Liberals were beginning to have some effect.

The relationship between State and individual

With these reforms, the State expanded its influence into areas previously left to the family, such as the provision of children's meals and child welfare as well as support for the elderly poor. The State also extended its influence into the labour market, laying down minimum wages in certain trades and minimum working conditions in others. Through the School Medical Service and the medical provisions of the National Insurance Act, the State moved into the area of health provision. All these forms of State action were moving away from the 19th century principle of laissez-faire. During the period down to 1951, this growth in State intervention was to be taken much further.

The State also took new powers of compulsion over the individual. National insurance compelled large numbers of workers and their employers to contribute to the schemes against unemployment and sickness, while employers in certain trades had to pay a minimum wage. The principle of a 'non-contributory' pension paid for out of general taxation through the Post Office, independently from the Poor Law, was established. This moved provision for the poor from the local community to central government. The two National Insurance Acts introduced the principle and practice of social insurance to Britain. This began to replace a multiplicity of local and voluntary schemes with a compulsory national one. The financing of pensions and national insurance also established the idea of using general taxation to redistribute income from one section of society to another. However, there were limits to this State involvement. The reforms before 1908 were significantly less radical than those after 1908 and much legislation involved local authorities rather than the central State directly.

Child legislation was often permissive rather than compulsory, although this was changing by 1914. New Liberals like Lloyd George and Churchill believed there should be limits to State intervention. They did not want the State to take over industry or to provide all services for its

Activity

Group activity

Divide into three groups:

■ Group 1 considers reforms to help children.

■ Group 2 considers reforms to help workers.

■ Group 3 considers reforms to help the elderly and sick.

Each group should assess the extent to which their section of society was helped by the Liberal welfare reforms.

PUNCH, OR THE LONDON CHARIVARI.—August 5, 1908.

THE PHILANTHROPIC HIGHWAYMAN.

Mr. Lloyd-George. *"I'LL MAKE 'EM PITY THE AGED POOR!"*

Fig. 6 *Cartoon by Edward L. Sambourne in 'Punch' depicting the Chancellor of the Exchequer, David Lloyd George*

■ **Activity**

Talking point

The issue of the relationship between the State and the individual raises some important concerns. Consider the following:

1 How far should a State interfere in people's personal lives?

2 Is interference justified in certain cases?

3 How did the Liberals' interventions differ from State intervention in the present day?

Divide into groups and decide on your responses to these questions. Then share your views with the rest of your class.

■ **Key terms**

Constitution: a system of government including fundamental principles; the basic laws by which a country is governed.

Budget: this has been presented to the House of Commons by the Chancellor of the Exchequer every year since the 1690s. It summarises what the government intends to spend money on in the coming year and also how it intends to raise that money. These proposals have then to be accepted by parliament before changes in taxation can be made. The budget is presented for approval to firstly the House of Commons, then the House of Lords and finally the monarch before it becomes law.

Chancellor of the Exchequer: the minister directly responsible for the government's finances and indirectly responsible for the nation's finances. The Chancellor is the second most important person in the government, after the prime minister.

citizens. Their reforms were not universal, and were largely based on personal contributions.

Of course, the cause of reform was not helped by the opposition of the House of Lords or the continued presence of 'Old Liberals' in the government. Comparing the Liberal social reforms to those which came later in the 20th century, reveals continuity with the past rather than any radical break. The Liberal reforms still had many features of the 19th century, such as the Victorian distinction between the poor who deserved help and those who did not deserve it because of their misbehaviour. In many ways, the reforms were conservative rather than radical.

Constitutional and political reform

Although the Liberal governments of 1906–14 are most famous for their social reforms, at the time it was their political and constitutional reforms that caused the most tension and debate. Between 1909 and 1911, there occurred perhaps the greatest constitutional crisis of the 20th century over the power of the House of Lords, while in the summer of 1914 political reform threatened to bring Ireland to the brink of civil war.

The years 1909–11 saw a serious clash between the Conservative-dominated House of Lords and the Liberal-dominated House of Commons. This clash resulted in two general elections in 1910 and eventually in the Parliament Act 1911. There were two stages to the crisis. The first was in 1909–10 over the 'People's Budget'; the second came in 1910–11 over the Parliament Act.

The political complexion of the Lords did not always match that of the majority in the Commons, since membership of the Lords was hereditary while the Commons were elected. Since 1886, the Lords had been dominated by the Conservatives. This had caused no problems during the periods of Conservative rule, 1886–92 and 1895–1905, but when the Liberals had a majority in the Commons, the Lords could use their power to wreck their opponents' legislation. This had happened during the Liberal government of 1892–5 when dozens of 'backwoodsmen' who never normally bothered to attend the Lords suddenly appeared to vote against the Liberals' proposals to give Home Rule to Ireland.

After the Liberal landslide of 1906, the Conservatives were powerless in the Commons, with less than a quarter of the seats, but the Conservative leaders, Balfour and Lord Lansdowne (who led the Conservatives in the Lords) decided to use the permanent Conservative majority in the Lords to block the policies of the new Liberal government. The House of Lords became 'Mr Balfour's poodle'. As long as this continued, the Conservatives could still continue to rule. Balfour even claimed that 'the great Unionist (Conservative) party should still control, whether in government or in opposition, the destinies of the British Empire'. In 1906, the Liberals' Education Bill was so mutilated by the Lords that it had to be abandoned. Other Liberal measures blocked by the Lords were a Scottish Land Bill, the Abolition of Plural Voting Bill and the Licensing Bill of 1908.

The first constitutional crisis: the People's Budget 1909–10

In his 1909–10 **Budget**, Lloyd George, the **Chancellor of the Exchequer**, needed to find £15 million of extra revenue to provide for the new social services and for the construction of naval warships. He set out to tax the rich and especially those living on unearned income.

PUNCH, OR THE LONDON CHARIVARI.—February 24, 1909.

EDUCATION

LICENSING

HOUSE OF LORDS VETO

UNEMPLOYED

BUDGET

PREFERENTIAL TREATMENT.

"The expenditure of the year will be considerably in excess of that of the past twelve months . . . and in consequence less time than usual will, I fear, be available for the consideration of other legislative measures."—*The King's Speech.*

Fig. 7 *David Lloyd George, Chancellor of the Exchequer, wheeling his 'People's Budget' to the House of Commons. The prime minister, Asquith, in the guise of a policeman, holds up the traffic bearing various demands for funding. Cartoon by Edward L. Sambourne from 'Punch', London, 21 February 1909*

Lloyd George's Budget of April 1909 proposed:

■ increased incomes tax from one shilling to one shilling and two pence in the pound on incomes over £3,000 a year

■ a new super tax on incomes over £5,000 a year

average income in £160

■ increased death duties on estates of over £5,000 a year

■ new land taxes. The first was taxation of the 'unearned increment of land value'. This was an increase in value that was not the result of improvement by the landowner but the result of greater demand for land. It was a tax on the profits made by capitalists and speculators by the mere possession of land. It put a duty of 20 per cent on the unearned increase in land value when it changed hands by sale or inheritance. The second was a duty of ½d in the pound on the value of undeveloped land and minerals. This was designed to hit those who held back their land from development in the hope of greater profits in the future.

ARMS RACE WITH GERMANY.

■ Questions

1 Which aspects of the budget do you imagine would cause most controversy?

2 Why is Lloyd George sometimes accused of launching a 'class war'?

■ Exploring the detail

Understanding taxes

■ Direct taxes are taxes on income. Income tax is the clearest example.

■ Earned income is income from the wages, salaries and fees that individuals earn each year.

■ Income tax is a tax on all forms of income calculated at so many pence in the pound.

■ Unearned income is income derived from sources other than the individual's direct own labour. This might be income from investments and rents from land.

■ Indirect taxes are taxes on spending rather than income. Taxes are paid when the individual buys something.

■ Key terms

Redistributive taxation: a taxation that not only raises money but takes money from the relatively well off to provide help for the relatively poor.

Progressive taxation: a taxation that takes a larger proportion of high incomes than of low incomes.

Money bill: a bill involving the raising or spending of money. A finance bill.

Peers: members of the House of Lords, which was sometimes called the House of Peers.

■ indirect taxes on luxury goods such as motor cars and petrol but also on beer and tobacco. ~ Wk.Cl.

Lloyd George needed to increase revenue and he favoured the redistribution of wealth from rich to poor, but probably had other reasons for launching this provocative Budget too. He wanted to show working-class voters that they need not vote for the new Labour Party in order to get radical measures and, still more importantly, he wanted to punish the Conservatives for their opposition in the Lords. If Lloyd George set out to provoke the House of Lords so as to give the Liberal government the excuse to curb their powers, he certainly succeeded.

The land taxes were especially controversial. They would not produce a great deal of tax revenue, but they certainly inflamed Conservative landowners. A Budget Protest League was set up and denounced the taxes as confiscation and robbery. Lloyd George was ready for the fight. In his Limehouse speech of July 1909, he spoke of the opposition to his proposals being a 'class war'. CLASS WAR

> It is disgraceful for a rich country like ours to allow those who have toiled all their days, to end their lives penniless and possibly near starvation. Have you been down a coal mine? I went down one the other day. We sank down into a pit half a mile deep and we had three-quarters of a mile of rock and shale above us. You could see the pit-props bend. Sometimes they give way and there is mutilation and death. Often a spark ignites and the whole pit is deluged in fire. In the colliery next to the one I visited, 300 people lost their lives in that way. Yet, when I knock on the doors of the landlords and say, 'You know those poor fellows who have been digging at the risk of their lives – and are now broken and can earn no more. Won't you give something towards keeping them out of the workhouse?' They scowl and say 'Only a ha-penny' and then they turn their dogs on us.

2   *Adapted extract from Lloyd George's speech at Limehouse, July 1909*

The Conservatives argued that this was no ordinary Budget because it amounted to a social revolution. Opponents of the Budget were worried by the idea of **redistributive taxation** and also of **progressive taxation**. They feared that once these principles were established they could be extended to 'soak the rich' and even out the very unfair distribution of income and wealth in Edwardian Britain. In November 1909, in an unprecedented vote, the Lords rejected or 'vetoed' the Budget. The convention that the Lords should not interfere with '**money bills**' was broken and the Liberal government was left with no legal authority to collect taxes. They had no choice but to call a general election in January 1910 on the issue.

The general election of January 1910

The Liberals tried to fight the election on the issue of whether Britain should be governed by a majority of elected MPs in the House of Commons or by non-elected, hereditary **peers** in the House of Lords. Lloyd George summarised this in his slogan 'The Peers versus the People'. Like most political slogans, it was not quite accurate – in 1910 less than half of British adults had the right to vote. Lloyd George launched a bitter campaign against the Lords depicting them as rich, selfish, unpatriotic men begrudging extra taxes for social reform.

Fig. 8 *David Lloyd George, Chancellor of the Exchequer, walking in central London with his close political colleague Winston Churchill shortly after the January 1910 election. The 'dynamic duo' are accompanied by Lloyd George's wife and his parliamentary aide*

What gives five hundred men the right to override the judgement of millions of people who are engaged in the industries which made the wealth of this country?

One man works throughout his life in grinding labour to earn money for his family, and when he is old and asks for a little pension he is accused of starting a revolution! Another man who does not work can receive more in unearned income every day than his poor neighbour earns in a whole year of toil! Where did that system come from?

 3 *Extract from a speech by Lloyd George in 1909*

The Conservatives suggested that there were other ways to raise the money, such as by tariffs on foreign imports, and that it was the duty of the House of Lords to restrain governments from making sweeping changes that the electorate had not voted on, but the Liberals won the 1910 election, even if only very narrowly. With 275 seats to the Conservatives' 273, they had a majority of two. The Irish Nationalists won 82 seats and the Labour Party 40. The Liberals therefore had to depend on Irish support to pass the budget and this they were willing to give, in return for an attack on the powers of the House of Lords. They were keen to see the Lords weakened so that they could achieve their desire for Home Rule for Ireland. As the Commons were able to show a majority for the Budget, endorsed by an election, the Lords at last agreed to pass the Budget.

The second constitutional crisis of 1910–11 and the Parliament Act of 1911

The Liberals were determined that the House of Lords should never again block a measure passed by the House of Commons. In 1910, they therefore drew up a bill to curb the power of the House of Lords by taking away its power of veto.

The 1910 Parliament Bill proposed that:

- the House of Lords was to have no power to amend or reject those bills that the speaker of the Commons (an impartial referee) certified to be true money bills
- the House of Lords was to have no power to reject (or veto) other legislation, but could delay it for no longer than two years. This was known as a 'suspensory veto'.
- the maximum period between general elections was to be reduced from seven years to five years.

Activity

Talking point

Hold a mock parliamentary session between the supporters and the opponents of the 1909 budget.

Fig. 9 *Drawing by S. Begg of the scene in the House of Lords on the passing of the Parliament Bill 1911*

This bill would easily pass the Commons, but the problem was that any law to curb the Lords' power would have to be passed by the Lords themselves.

Asquith's solution was to ask King Edward VII (who had the power to create peers) to promise to create enough Liberal peers to outvote the Conservative peers in the Lords. However, Edward VII died suddenly in May 1910 and the new king, George V, tried to get the Liberals and Conservatives to agree a solution without resorting to the creation of new peers. A Constitutional Conference was held between June and November 1910. The Conservatives offered to reform the composition of the Lords, but the Liberals were determined to reduce its constitutional powers.

The Conservatives also tried to insist that the Lords should, at least, have the right to veto any change in the constitution (which would enable them to keep on blocking Home Rule for Ireland) unless the electorate approved such a change in a **referendum**. On this issue, the conference broke down. Asquith was under strong Irish pressure to reject the Conservatives' proposal. George V finally agreed that he would create enough new peers to pass the Parliament Bill, as long as the Liberals won a general election fought on that issue. This second general election of 1910 was held in December.

Key term

Referendum: a vote of the people taken between elections when they are asked to say yes or no to a single issue of major importance.

Key profiles

Edward VII

King Edward VII was Queen Victoria's eldest son and succeeded her to the throne in 1901. The early 1900s are often called the 'Edwardian era' after him. He died in 1910.

George V

King George V became king in 1910, reigning until 1936. His reign saw several important political crises as well as the 1914–8 war.

The December 1910 general election

The December election left the Liberals and Conservatives with exactly the same number of seats, 272 each, but because they had support from Labour, who won 42 seats, and from the Irish Nationalists, who won 84 seats, the Liberals were able to rely on a working majority and could remain in government. In May 1911, the Commons passed the Parliament Bill. The next stage was up to the House of Lords.

The crisis reached its peak when the Lords passed wrecking amendments to the bill that the Commons rejected. Some Conservatives, nicknamed 'the rats', felt that they should cooperate with the bill; others, nicknamed 'the hedgers', led by Lord Lansdowne, were undecided; still others, nicknamed 'the ditchers' or 'diehards', led by Willoughby de Broke, were determined to oppose the Parliament Bill 'to the last ditch'. However, many Conservatives realised that the consequences of not passing the bill might be worse than those of accepting it.

In August 1911, the crucial reading of the Parliament Bill, without amendments, took place in the Lords. Most Conservative peers were 'hedgers' and abstained but enough 'rats' voted for the bill to outvote the 'ditchers'. By doing so, they avoided the Lords being swamped with newly-created Liberal peers. The Parliament Act became law – passed by 131 Liberals and Conservative 'rats' against 114 'diehards'. Balfour supported the 'hedgers' but the event so divided the Conservatives that Balfour was forced to resign the leadership in November 1911, when Andrew Bonar Law succeeded him as leader.

Key profile

Andrew Bonar Law

Andrew Bonar Law was born in Canada of Ulster and Scottish emigrant parents. He returned to Scotland working in the family iron business. Elected to parliament in 1900, he succeeded Balfour as leader of the Conservatives in 1911. Bonar Law vigorously supported the Ulster Unionists in their opposition to Home Rule. He was briefly prime minister in 1922–3 but illness forced him to resign. He is sometimes called 'the unknown prime minister'.

Assessing the impact of the Parliament Act

The Parliament Act helped make the British constitution more democratic. Never again could the Lords permanently over-ride the Commons and political power had shifted decisively to the lower house. There has, for example, never been a British prime minister sitting in the Lords since this date, although this nearly happened with Lord Halifax in May 1940. However, the Lords remained non-elected and retained their judicial function as the ultimate court of appeal. There was to be no major reform of the House of Lords until 1999.

Other political reforms

Some of the Liberals' reforms, such as the 1906 Workmen's Compensation Act and the 1906 Trade Disputes Act, were a direct result of the demands made by the Liberals' Labour allies. After the 1910 elections, when the Liberals were even more dependent on Labour because of their reduced majority in the Commons, they enacted two further reforms with far-reaching political consequences.

Labour demanded some redress after the Osborne court case of 1908–9 which threatened the existence of their party. Walter Osborne was a railway trade unionist who supported the Liberal Party. He objected to his trade union using some of his yearly subscription to help fund the Labour Party. His case went through to the House of Lords who ruled in his favour, declaring that it was illegal for a trade union to collect money for political purposes. The Osborne case was a major blow to the Labour Party which depended upon the trade unions for the money to pay its MPs, fund elections and run the party.

The Liberals remedied the situation by passing the Payment of MPs Act in 1911. Whereas, before 1911, members of parliament received no salary, so only those with a private income could afford to be MPs, this provided for State payment of MPs at £400 per year.

In addition, the Liberals passed a new Trade Union Act in 1913 that allowed unions to impose a 'political levy' as part of members' fees, provided that members could 'contract out'. Those trade unionists who did not wish to support the Labour Party financially could refuse to pay that part of their union subscription which the party received.

These acts helped widen representation in the Commons, allowing men of humble origins to stand as MPs. It also gave a huge boost to the Labour Party and ensured them of a steady flow of funds and a strong union backing. However, the Liberals did nothing to extend the vote, which was still denied to all females (and a fair number of males), despite the activities of the suffragettes and the Womens' Suffrage Union.

■ **Cross-reference**

The **suffragettes** and the women's **suffrage movement** are discussed on pages 46–7.

Political reform and the Third Irish Home Rule Bill 1912

Fig. 10 *Sir Edward Carson reviewing the Ulster volunteers*

After the December 1910 general election, the Liberals were dependent on the support of the 84 Irish Nationalist MPs in the Commons in order to stay in power. These MPs, led by John Redmond, wanted Irish Home Rule and believed that the 1911 Parliament Act had finally made this possible.

In 1912, the Third Home Rule Bill began its progress through parliament. It was a moderate measure that would give Ireland its own parliament with power to make laws on purely Irish matters, while the British parliament would keep control over foreign policy, defence, trade, pensions and national insurance. Under the terms of the bill, Ireland would continue to send MPs to Westminster.

Opposition to Home Rule

The Conservatives had long opposed Home Rule and supported the cause of the Ulster Unionists, Protestants of mainland descent living in the north-east corner of Ireland. Conservatives argued that Irish Home Rule would undermine Britain's great power status by breaking up the United Kingdom and the British Empire. They said that the Liberals had no authority to change the constitution of the UK because Home Rule had not been an issue in the 1910 elections. Unionists in Ireland feared discrimination in a Catholic-dominated country where there was a growing emphasis on the Gaelic heritage. Economically, Ulster was the only industrialised part of Ireland with a major shipbuilding and textile industry centred on Belfast. Ulster Protestants did not want to lose their control over this wealth and felt that Belfast had more in common with British cities like Glasgow or Liverpool than with Ireland's capital Dublin. Ulster businessmen did not want their industries taxed heavily to help the poorer, rural parts of Ireland.

Cross-reference

The issues surrounding **Irish Home Rule**, the role of **John Redmond**, and **Liberal policies** in this area before 1912, including the First and Second Irish Home Rule Bills, are outlined on page 5.

Exploring the detail

Ireland's Gaelic heritage

The Gaelic heritage of Ireland was revived by Nationalists in the late-19th century as a way of demonstrating Ireland's separate identity from Great Britain. This cultural nationalism encouraged the speaking of Erse, the Gaelic language of Ireland, the playing of Gaelic sports such as hurling, the study of Irish history, poetry and literature.

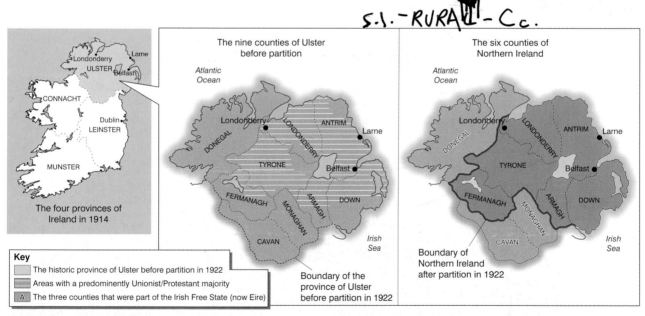

Fig. 11 *The counties of Ireland*

Before 1911 the Ulster Unionists had relied upon the House of Lords to veto any Home Rule bill but, with that power gone, they began to organise themselves to resist Home Rule under the leadership of the lawyer, Edward Carson. Carson organised meetings and drew up the Ulster **Covenant**, which thousands of Ulstermen signed, some in their own blood. In 1913, when the Home Rule Bill had passed the Commons but was held up in the Lords, Carson began to form an army – the Ulster Volunteer Force – to resist the imposition of an all-Irish parliament. In 1914, his supporters smuggled 30,000 rifles and 3 million rounds of ammunition into the Irish port of Larne. Despite such activities, the new Conservative leader, Andrew Bonar Law, offered the Ulster Unionists his support. Furthermore, in the 'Curragh Mutiny'

Key term

Covenant: a solemn, sacred agreement. In 1912, the Ulster Unionists drew up a written covenant which over 200,000 Ulstermen publicly signed in Belfast town hall. Its purpose was to frighten off the Liberal government's attempt to put Ulster under the authority of a Home Rule parliament in Dublin.

Key term

Curragh: one of the main bases for the British Army in Ireland and scene of the so-called 'Curragh Mutiny' in March 1914. General Gough and 57 cavalry officers who had family connections in Ulster told their commanding officer that they would resign rather than be party to any attempt to force Home Rule on Ulster. The episode cast doubt on the Liberal government's ability to enforce Home Rule in Ulster if it became law.

of March 1914, British officers commanding British soldiers at the **Curragh** in Ireland threatened to resign rather than fight against this Ulster Unionist resistance.

Key profile

Sir Edward Carson

Sir Edward Carson became the leader of Protestant Ulster in its struggle against Home Rule. Ironically, he was a famous Dublin lawyer who had led the prosecution in the trial of Oscar Wilde. He was a passionate believer in the Union between Great Britain and Ireland and between 1912 and 1914 he led the Ulster Unionist resistance to Home Rule. Along with his colleague James Craig, he organised mass demonstrations, led the signing of the Ulster Covenant and encouraged the formation of the Ulster Volunteer Force. Carson played a crucial role in ensuring that Ulster remained part of the United Kingdom.

The Irish Nationalists countered these developments by forming a militia of their own – the Irish Volunteers – to enforce Home Rule. In the summer of 1914, they too managed to smuggle in rifles and ammunition, creating fears of a civil war in Ireland.

The Home Rule Bill was due to become law in the autumn of 1914, following the two-year delay imposed by the Lords. Last minute talks between the parties at Buckingham Palace failed to reach an agreement but civil war was averted when the outbreak of war against Germany in Europe led to the suspension of Home Rule for the duration of that war. The Irish problem was suspended, but not resolved.

A closer look

The Liberal Party – the start of its decline

After 1915, the Liberals never formed a government again and after 1922 no Liberal held major political office.

In 1935, George Dangerfield suggested that this decline was already underway in the late-19th century but accelerated between 1910 and 1914. Dangerfield felt that the quarrel with the House of Lords, the threats from Ulster Unionists, the sufragettes' attacks on the government and the growing power of militant trade unionism all weakened Liberalism so much that it was unable to survive the terrible strains imposed on it by the Great War. Similarly, Trevor Wilson likened the Liberals to a man who, despite symptoms of illness remained active but then fell under a runaway bus, i.e. the Great War, and never recovered.

However, historians such as P. Clarke have argued that Liberalism was revitalising itself before 1914. New Liberalism and the reforms it helped inspire suggest that the Liberals were adapting to the changes of the early-20th century and laying foundations for future developments. Clarke points to Liberal success in by-elections in industrial areas like Lancashire right down to the Great War and the further reforms planned for 1915. Both the constitutional crisis of 1909–11 and the threat of civil war in Ireland were contained, whilst militant trade unionism and suffragette violence were losing support by 1914. Though the Liberals had lost their majority in 1910, they continued to be a match for the Conservatives. Shrewd Liberals realised that they also needed to compete with the rising Labour Party, but there is no evidence of a Liberal loss of faith in themselves before 1914.

Learning outcomes

Through your study of this section you should understand why the Liberals came to dominate government after 1906 and the reasons for the many social, constitutional and political reforms which they enacted. You should, in particular, be aware of the extent of poverty in Britain in the early-20th century and how far the Liberal reforms went towards addressing this.

You should also be able to explain the meaning and impact of New Liberalism and appreciate the changes that took place in government and in the relationship between the State and the people in the years 1906–14.

Through a careful consideration of the material presented in this section, you should be able to provide a supported judgement about the extent of Liberal success in a variety of areas.

 Examination-style questions

(a) Explain why the House of Lords rejected
the 1909 Budget. *(12 marks)*

 Questions that ask 'Explain why' require an answer that consists of a series of reasons. These reasons need to be linked and, ideally, prioritised to show that you have reached a judgement regarding their relative importance. To answer this question, you will need to consider the arguments used by supporters and opponents. A good answer will mention the Lords had been using their veto before 1909 and the attitude of Conservative leaders towards the Upper House.

(b) How successful was the Liberal government in
dealing with the constitutional crisis of 1909–11? *(24 marks)*

 Questions asking 'How successful' require an assessment of the degree to which aims and objectives were achieved. You should avoid a description of what happened. Instead, balance the evidence for success with consideration of the limitations and any areas of failure. You will need to consider the degree of Liberal success in relation to the budget, the Lords' position and powers, the general elections of 1910 and the long-term effects of the 1911 Act.

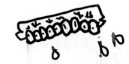

3 Britain and the First World War

Fig. 1 *British troops man-handling a captured German field gun amidst the carnage of the Western Front*

In this chapter you will learn about:

- how the Liberal government led Britain through the First World War

- the impact of the war on the political parties

- the economic impact of the war

- the extent of social change by 1918

- the extent to which the war was responsible for accelerating women's political emancipation.

Key term

Western Front: the main area of British land fighting in the 1914–8 war. It comprised part of Belgium, Flanders, and northern France as far as Switzerland.

The Great War

'Good-morning; good-morning!' the General said
When we met him last week on our way to the line.
Now the soldiers he smiled at are most of 'em dead,
And we're cursing his staff for incompetent swine.
'He's a cheery old card', grunted Harry to Jack
As they slogged up to Arras with rifle and pack.

But he did for them both by his plan of attack.

1   *'The General', Siegfried Sassoon*

Siegfried Sassoon's famous poem portrays the enduring image of the First World War, and its horrific loss of life in a new form of warfare. The Great War, as people at the time called it, is often seen as a tragic waste of young lives in the trenches on the **Western Front** – a war in which 'Lions were led by Donkeys'. This idea of idealistic young men (the Lions) being sacrificed by the callous and incompetent tactics of upper-class officers (the Donkeys) has been immortalised in the collective memory by poets like Sassoon and Wilfred Owen, by Joan Littlewood's satirical musical *Oh What a Lovely War!* and even by *Blackadder Goes Forth*. Some may believe that the war exposed the deep class divisions that had existed in 1914 and led to greater equality. This, in turn, links with another idea – the apparent transformation in the roles and status of women as a result of the impact of the war.

The First World War was actually two parallel European wars, one in the West and one in the East. The conflict is misleadingly called a world war because it involved the colonial empires of the European powers and because the United States entered the war in 1917. The war did indeed bring about revolutionary changes. It led to the overthrow of the old empires of Imperial Germany, Austria-Hungary, Tsarist Russia and Ottoman Turkey; and to the creation of many new national States. It led to the first-ever Communist State, in Soviet Russia. It led to massive changes in the world economy, in intellectual ideas and in the way people lived their lives. Not all of these changes directly affected Britain. Many of them did, however, and it is important to assess the precise impact of the Great War on politics, the economy and society in Britain.

■ Key chronology
The five-minute history of the First World War

1914
War of illusions   When it began in 1914, Britain was allied to France and Tsarist Russia, fighting against the 'central powers' – Germany, Austria-Hungary and Turkey. All the main powers expected a short, decisive war. It was only by the end of 1914 that it became apparent the war was going to be a long costly stalemate.

1915
The new warfare   It took a long time to adjust to the huge demands for armaments and manpower needed for this new, industrialised form of warfare. Through most of 1915, the warring powers were building up their war efforts.

1916
Deadlock   There were massive battles involving millions of men – at Verdun and the Somme on the Western Front, on the Eastern Front, and also at sea in the Battle of Jutland. Despite huge loss of life (necessitating the introduction of conscription in Britain), the war remained deadlocked.

1917
Cracking under the strain   The strains of war brought the participants close to collapse. The Russian Revolution ended the rule of the tsars. Similar collapse threatened the Austrian and Ottoman Empires. Britain and France were struggling to keep their economies going. The western allies could only carry on the war effectively because of American entry into the war.

1918
The collapse of the central powers   The entry of the United States decided the outcome of the war. By the autumn of 1918, the central powers could not fight on. The Austrian and Ottoman Empires fell apart. Germany surrendered. Britain and France had 'won the war' – but both were badly damaged economically.

■ Key chronology
The Liberal government and the First World War

1914	Liberal government led by Asquith.
1914 August	Outbreak of war, BEF sent to France.
1914 October	Parliament passes Defence of the Realm Act (DORA).
1915 May	First war coalition formed with Conservatives.
1915 June	Ministry of Munitions set up under Lloyd George.
1916 January	First Military Service Act, bringing in conscription.
1916 April	Easter Rising in Dublin.
1916 July	Start of the Battle of the Somme.
1916 December	Lloyd George replaces Asquith as prime minister.
1917	Second war coalition under Lloyd George. Severe shipping losses due to German U-boat campaigns. Increasing divisions within Liberal Party.
1917 April	American entry into the war.
1918 February	Representation of the People Act extends the Franchise.
1918 May	Maurice Debate causes Liberal Party open split.
1918 November	End of hostilities after German surrender.
1918 December	'Coupon election'.

■ The political and economic impact of the First World War on Britain, 1914–8

The political impact of the war

Asquith's Liberal government faced enormous tasks in 1914, especially when it gradually became clear the war would be a long one. To win such a war Britain needed manpower and materials, and the government also

These are covered in the Introduction and Chapters 1 and 2.

Activity

Thinking point

Traditional liberal beliefs included:

- ■ 'laissez-faire'
- ■ Free Trade
- ■ balanced budgets
- ■ limited State intervention
- ■ internationalism
- ■ freedom of the individual.

These are covered in the Introduction and Chapters 1 and 2. Explain each of these and assess how and why each was undermined by the demands of war.

Key terms

Shell shortage: refers to the crisis in production of ammunition, which was now being used in massive quantities on the Western Front. Politicians and military men were blamed for letting this situation happen.

Munitions: weapons and ammunition needed for the Armed Forces.

Coalition: several political parties working together to form a government.

Maurice Debate: in February 1918 this arose out of a letter to *The Times* newspaper by General Maurice, the former Director of Military Operations, claiming that the government had lied about the strength of the British Army in France in early 1918. This came at a time when the German armies seemed about to break the allied lines. Its real importance, however, was that it divided the Liberal Party in parliament.

Fig. 2 *First World War recruitment poster by Baden-Powell illustrating the concept of 'total war'*

had to maintain national unity and morale. The strains of the war put great pressure on politicians of all parties.

The Liberal Party

The Liberal government continued to lead the country until May 1915, but the war produced tensions within the party because it undermined many traditional Liberal beliefs, particularly those relating to the freedom of the individual.

The '**shell shortage**' in May 1915 forced the Liberal government into a much greater extension of State power in order to produce the level of **munitions** needed for victory. Asquith found it hard to give up principles such as laissez-faire but Lloyd George, who was appointed Minister of Munitions in 1915, realised that the State must take extensive powers over the economy if the war was to be won. By 1915, the Liberals also had to give up the idea of ruling alone. Asquith had to take the decision, which horrified many Liberals and their Irish Nationalist allies, to form a war **coalition** including Conservative and Labour politicians.

Asquith retained the unity of the Liberals until 1916, when he was replaced as prime minister by Lloyd George. Thereafter, splits in the party widened and the party split during the **Maurice Debate** of 1918. When Lloyd George continued the coalition with Conservatives beyond the end of the war, it allowed a Conservative revival, while the Labour Party replaced the Liberals as the party of reform. The Liberals never wholly recovered and the party went into rapid decline after the war.

A closer look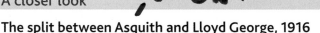

The split between Asquith and Lloyd George, 1916

The government experienced a number of setbacks in 1916. There was the Easter Rising of Irish Republicans in Dublin, the failure of the navy to defeat the German battle fleet in the inconclusive naval Battle of Jutland, and the terrible casualties suffered by British forces in the Battle of the Somme, as Britain tried to relieve the pressure on their French allies on the Western Front. All these setbacks increased criticism of Asquith's leadership. In contrast, Lloyd George, who had been moved from his post as Minister of Munitions to become Minister of War, was applauded for his drive and energy. Lloyd George argued strongly for conscription to be used more extensively. He also demanded the formation of an inner war cabinet, from which Asquith was to be excluded. Asquith refused to accept these changes. The political negotiations about re-organising the war coalition, held at Buckingham Palace, broke down. On 7 December 1916, Lloyd George was appointed prime minister. This split the Liberal Party. Most Liberal MPs followed Asquith into opposition but about 100 gave their support to Lloyd George. As soon as he became prime minister, Lloyd George formed the second war coalition. This gave much more power to the Conservatives, who filled the majority of cabinet posts. Lloyd George was now supported by only half the parliamentary Liberal Party. Although no one realised this at the time, there would never again be a Liberal government – or even a government that was predominantly Liberal.

The Conservative Party

Although politically weak at the beginning of the war, the Conservatives gained political momentum from it. By 1914, Conservative opposition to the Liberal government had grown particularly intense over Irish Home Rule; the outbreak of the Great War got them out of the embarrassing position of seeming to support armed rebellion in Ulster. The Conservatives directed their energies to supporting the war effort. In 1915, they joined Asquith's new war coalition. Serving in the coalition government, even under Liberal leadership, revived Conservative fortunes. Indeed, they found it easier to fit in than the Liberals did, with the emphasis of the war years on patriotism, militarism and closeness to the empire.

The Labour Party

The Labour Party almost split in 1914 over whether it should support the war. The Labour Party essentially believed in the international cooperation of the working class and was opposed to war and militarism. Some leaders, like Ramsay MacDonald, refused to compromise and support the war and were mercilessly criticised in the press. However, most of the Labour movement did support the war. In 1916, Arthur Henderson became the first-ever Labour politician to be given a place in the cabinet.

Cross-reference
The **crisis in Ireland** is detailed on pages 30–2.
The **Defence of the Realm Act**, or **DORA**, is explained on page 40.

The **crisis in Ireland** is detailed on pages 30–2.

The **Defence of the Realm Act**, or **DORA**, is explained on page 40.

Key profile

Ramsay MacDonald

The illegitimate son of a Scottish farm worker, Ramsay MacDonald was one of the founders of the Labour Party. He was Secretary of the Labour Party before the Great War, negotiated the 'Lib-Lab' Pact in 1903 and became leader of the party in 1911. During the war, his pacifism meant that he had to resign as leader but he became leader again in 1922. In 1923, he became the first Labour prime minister, and was elected again in 1929. After 1931, however, MacDonald was regarded as a traitor, because of his decision to form a National government with the Conservatives. His greatest contribution was to convince the country that Labour was a respectable alternative to the Conservatives and Liberals.

The cooperation of the trade unions, the backbone of the Labour Party, was recognised as vital to the war effort. One of Labour's leading figures, Arthur Henderson, was given a post in the war cabinet itself. Trade union membership doubled during and immediately after the war, reaching 8 million. The war also led to the widening of the franchise. This ensured that all men would have the parliamentary vote at the next general election, so giving Labour the prospect of much bigger electoral support from the working class. Overall, the war encouraged ideas of equality, because everyone had suffered and everyone had contributed to the war effort. In its new constitution of 1918, the Labour Party committed itself to openly 'socialist' ideas.

CLOSE 4. - NOW committed to Marx ideologies.

■ Cross-reference

The **Labour split** in 1931 and the setting up of the **National government** are covered on pages 70–1.

■ Key profile

Arthur Henderson

Arthur Henderson was a trade unionist and Labour MP. When he was brought into the war coalition government to represent the Labour movement in 1915, he became the first Labour MP to sit in the cabinet. In 1916, he became part of the small, inner war cabinet. He resigned in 1917 and played a key role in drafting the Labour Party's new constitution of 1918. In the 1920s, he held posts in the two Labour governments. Though a moderate, he refused to follow MacDonald into the National government. After MacDonald's expulsion from the Labour Party he became temporary leader.

Fig. 3 *Effects of the fighting in Dublin following the Easter Rising, 1916*

The Irish Nationalist Party

For the Irish Nationalist Party, the war was a disaster. The coming of war had put their long-awaited Home Rule 'on hold' and between 1916 and 1918 they were increasingly overtaken in popularity in Ireland by the more extreme Sinn Fein party, which wanted complete independence from the rest of Britain, not merely Home Rule. In the 1918 general election, the Irish Nationalists were overwhelmingly defeated by Sinn Fein, which won 73 out of 108 Irish seats. Sinn Fein stood for the complete separation of all of Ireland, including Ulster, from Great Britain and was prepared to use force to achieve it. Some Sinn Fein members took part in the republican rising in Dublin at Easter 1916, and the violent suppression of this rising by British troops led many moderate Irish voters to switch their allegiance to Sinn Fein. From 1919 onwards, its armed wing, the Irish Republican Army, fought the British.

The 'coupon election' of 1918

At the end of the war, the personal rivalry between Asquith and Lloyd George dominated British politics. Lloyd George was very popular in the country, but most of the Liberal Party's funds and its organisation in the constituencies were under Asquith's control. Lloyd George chose to fight the first post-war election in collaboration with the Conservatives. He promised that, if elected, he would form a peacetime coalition government, including the Conservatives. Those who fought the election in support of the formation of this coalition were given a certificate signed by Lloyd George and the Conservative leader, Bonar Law – this certificate was nicknamed a 'coupon'. Thus, at the 1918 election, voters had to choose between two rival Liberal parties.

By the time of the election, the Representation of the People Act had been passed, extending the vote to a wider section of society than before. The Lloyd George or 'coupon' Liberals did quite well, winning 133 seats. Asquith's independent Liberals did badly, winning only 28 seats. Asquith himself lost his seat. The Labour Party made important gains, with 63 seats and 2.4 million votes in total. The Conservatives were the main winners, with 333 seats. Their success was not only due to the 'coupon' factor but also to the nationalistic mood in the country in December 1918.

State intervention

The influence of the State on people's lives grew enormously in the war years. Government gained unprecedented powers – to conscript men for armed service; to censor any material it believed might aid the enemy; to ration food; and to fix prices, wages, profits and rents.

Before 1914, Britain, unlike many European countries, did not conscript men to serve in the armed forces but relied upon men volunteering to serve. 'Voluntarism' remained the basis of recruitment until 1916. However, before 1914 the British Army had been small, only about 250,000. Between 1914 and 1916, voluntarism was remarkably successful in raising men. Some 2 million volunteered, producing one of the largest volunteer armies in history by 1916. Recruitment posters and propaganda encouraged young men to join up by playing on a variety of emotions – pride, patriotism and fear of embarrassment.

Voluntarism, however, could not supply new recruits in sufficient numbers to enable the government to meet the needs of the army, or plan for the needs of industry. Asquith's Liberal government continued to resist conscription but, in January 1916, the first Military Service Act was brought in for single men between the ages of 18 and 41. Following the terrible casualties on the Somme in the summer of 1916, a second Military Service Act extended conscription to married men. In February 1918, with Russia pulling out of the war and Germany about to switch millions of soldiers to the Western Front, a third act came in extending the age limits to 50. Thus, conscription significantly limited the freedom of the individual and gave the State power over life and death. Men refusing to join up could be imprisoned; if they were already in the army and refused to fight, they could be court martialled and shot. This was a major change in the relationship between the State and the individual.

State intervention was also necessary to gain the cooperation of the trade unions. At first, it was not certain that organised

Activity

Revision exercise

Using the information in this chapter, copy and complete the table below.

Summary of the Great War's effect on British political parties

Parties	1914	1918
Liberals		
Conservatives		
Labour		
Irish Nationalist		

Fig. 4 *An emotive, hard-hitting, First World War recruitment poster*

Daddy, what did *YOU* do in the Great War?

Key terms

Dilution agreements: agreements between the government and trade unions in various industries to allow semi-skilled, unskilled and women workers to be trained to do jobs, or parts of jobs, previously reserved for skilled craftsmen. These agreements from 1915 onwards were particularly important for the increased output of munitions.

Plural votes: in this period it was possible for men to have more than one vote if, for example, they lived in one constituency but had a business property in another constituency. Graduates of Oxford and Cambridge universities also had a vote for MPs elected by these bodies.

Defence of the Realm Act (DORA): the legal basis for the huge extension of State power during the war years. Passed originally by parliament in 1914, it was subsequently extended at various intervals during the war.

Activity

Revision exercise

Write a political speech which might have been given by an opponent of change during the war years. Warn of the dangers involved in excessive State intervention in the lives of people in Britain.

Cross-reference

Details of the **1918 Representation of the People Act**, which gave the right to vote to more people, and of **women's contribution to the war effort** are covered on pages 35–9.

labour would support what some denounced as a 'capitalist war' and there were some anti-war demonstrations in 1914. Soon, however, it became obvious that almost all workers supported the war effort. As Minister of Munitions, Lloyd George made demands on the trade unions known as **dilution agreements** in order to maximise the output of war materials. Trade unions were expected to work closely with employers and to avoid strikes. In turn, the trade unions demanded State controls on profits and rents, safeguards so workers would get their old jobs back when the war was over, and exemption of highly-skilled workers from conscription.

Cooperation between trade unions, employers and government was not always harmonious. In 1915 there was a major strike on Clydeside; and another in South Wales in 1917. Nevertheless, the number of working days lost through strikes fell from 10 million in 1913 to under 3 million by 1916. Overall, the war enhanced the status of trade unions. Governments now had to recognise their importance. Through their financing of the Labour Party, the unions became an important force in post-war politics.

Changes in the electoral system

Before 1918, the franchise or right to vote had been based on property, residence and gender. Britain was far from being a mass democracy in 1914. Because of the property and residence qualifications, 500,000 men had **plural votes**. Between 25 per cent and 40 per cent of men (and 100 per cent of women) did not qualify for the vote at all. More than half the adult population was disenfranchised. The Great War brought important changes for the electorate. It was recognised that it was wrong to have compulsory military service and yet have a large percentage of men unable to vote in parliamentary elections. Similarly, the parties had to recognise the contribution of women to the war effort and agree to extend the franchise at least to some women.

The State and the economy

The size of the war effort required State intervention on a huge scale, moving away from the former emphasis on 'laissez-faire'. In 1914, the government line was 'business as usual', but by 1918 the State was virtually running the whole economy.

Britain had to support a massive increase in the production of weapons of war. Two million shells had been produced by early 1915; by 1918, overall shell production had climbed to 187 million. The supply of machine guns went up from 270 in 1914 to 120,870 in 1918. Britain also had to supply vast quantities of war materials to its allies. There were also huge demands to provide transport, to increase and protect the provision of food and to ensure there were adequate supplies of fuel, above all coal.

The huge demand posed by war pushed up prices and created shortages of both materials and workers in 1914. Private industry could not cope on its own and the State began commandeering stocks of vital war materials and fixing prices. This began especially after the failure of the Neuve Chapelle offensive in 1915, the first major assault by British forces against the German defences in the West, a failure which many people at the time blamed on a shortage of shells. Lloyd George persuaded parliament to grant more State powers over industry by extending the **Defence of the Realm Act (DORA)** and he successfully campaigned for a Ministry of Munitions to oversee the purchase, production and supply of all war materials. He was appointed to head this new ministry himself.

The Ministry of Munitions set up a central purchasing system for buying essential war materials. It organised British science to help the war effort and encouraged the development and production of new weapons such as mortars and the tank. It encouraged factories to convert from peacetime to war production and also built its own national factories, some of which became huge enterprises. One in Leeds employed 16,000 workers producing 25 million shells a year by the end of the war. Key industries came under State control, such as railways, docks and coal mines. By 1918, the Ministry of Munitions directly managed 250 State factories, supervised another 20,000 factories and controlled almost 4 million workers. Women were encouraged to enter jobs previously done only by men. The munitions ministry controlled prices, wages and profits; rationed essential foods; bought 90 per cent of all imports and had charge of transport and fuel. The State altered the clocks by introducing British Summer Time, reduced the strength of alcoholic drinks and limited opening hours for public houses.

Fig. 5 *Young women filling shells in a munitions factory, wearing masks and gloves to stop inhalation and absorption of harmful chemicals. Male supervisors look on*

It was not only in manufacturing industry that the State intervened. The huge armies being assembled had to be fed, but this was difficult with a shortage of labour on the land and German **U-boats** sinking merchant ships bringing food from overseas. A Department of Food Production was set up to increase the amount of home grown foodstuffs. The government subsidised farmers to plough up wasteland, allocated scarce fertilisers, supplied prisoners of war to work on the land and encouraged women to volunteer for farm work.

The cost of the Great War was staggering. Government spending went up from £200 million in 1913 to £2,600 million in 1918. Traditionally, governments were supposed to 'balance the budget' but this had to be abandoned. Instead, the government had to borrow money from its own people and from neutral countries. During the war, Britain's national debt increased by 1,200 per cent. As well as borrowing, governments had also to increase taxation, both on the affluent middle classes and on manual workers. Income tax was greatly extended in 1915.

The war also created massive disruption to existing patterns of trade. Many traditional export markets were blocked off, hurting profits badly. Many imports ceased to be available, or else became vastly more expensive. Attacks on shipping meant vital cargoes were lost at sea. All this meant that new markets had to be opened up and new purchasing power had to be found. One obvious solution was to rely on the growing economic power of the United States.

Britain bought huge amounts of war material from American suppliers, much of it financed through the New York banking firm, J. P. Morgan. By late-1915, British financial reserves were running out. A loan was agreed giving Britain $5,000 million. Financial dependence on the United States became more and more crucial to Britain's war effort. The war was costing Britain $5 million per day, of which $2 million was raised in the United States. In December 1916, a secret report to King

> ### Key term
>
> **U-boats:** literally 'under sea boats', these were a form of submarine built by the German navy to sink British ships, both merchant and war ships.

Fig. 6 *American First World War poster offering support to Britain depicted as 'John Bull'*

George V warned that Britain faced bankruptcy and complete reliance on the United States. It was at this time that Asquith was replaced as prime minister by Lloyd George. 'We are going to lose this war' said Lloyd George in a pessimistic private moment. Britain did not lose the war – but, when war ended in 1918, Britain was facing severe economic difficulties and huge debt.

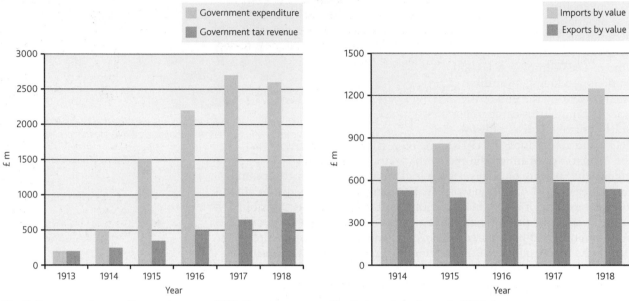

Fig. 7 *Government expenditure and revenue, 1913–8*

Fig. 8 *Imports and exports, 1914–8*

■ Activity

Statistical analysis

Study Figures 7 and 8. What financial problems for the government are revealed by these statistics? From the other evidence in this chapter, suggest how these problems were overcome.

■ Cross-reference

The **Second World War** and its **impact on society** during 1939–45 is discussed on pages 102–7.

■ Social change as a consequence of the war

The Great War involved most of the adult population either directly or indirectly. About 6 million men served in Britain's armed forces during the course of the conflict. Millions of civilians had their lives affected by the economic and social changes that the war caused or accelerated. The First World War is sometimes described as a 'total war' – a war in which all available resources, human and non-human, are mobilised for the war effort. The 1914–8 war may not have been as 'total' as the Second World War of 1939–45, but it was on a vaster scale than any previous war in Britain's history. Obviously, the impact of war varied greatly between different regions and various sections of the community. There were many differences and exceptions, even within the same social class or same gender, so it is difficult to measure precisely the war's impact on values and attitudes.

Impact on social classes

For the working classes, the war brought full employment and created jobs for wives, daughters and older children as well as for the main breadwinner. Good money could be made. There were also controls on rents and on the prices of essential commodities. These factors, together with a limited amount of rationing of basic foodstuffs, meant that the percentage of the population in deep poverty was significantly reduced by the end of the war. The middle and upper classes, however, experienced a reduction in their living standards. Income tax rose and profits were limited. The landed classes were hit hard by the high death rate amongst junior officers, most of whom initially came from landed gentry families, and by having to meet additional taxes on land. Many landed estates had to be sold off – 25 per cent of land holdings in England were sold between 1917 and 1921.

The war increased social mobility but class divisions were not broken down. In female employment, for example, working-class girls went mainly into munitions, middle-class girls more into nursing or administration. In the armed forces, class divisions between officers and men remained clear cut. There was probably more social levelling within the working classes than between the working and the middle classes. However, the terrible death toll of the war created a common bond of suffering and loss that ran across all social classes and was later expressed in the war memorials and rituals of remembrance.

A closer look

Effect of the war on adult men

For men below the age of 40, the biggest impact of the war was military service and the emotional and physical trauma it brought. Of the 6 million men serving in the armed forces, 750,000 were killed and about 2 million wounded. From 1916 onwards, the State imposed conscription. The Official Secrets Act and the Defence of the Realm Act restricted freedom of information about the war whilst posters, newspapers and films provided a regular diet of State propaganda. Soldiers and workers alike faced many restrictions, even on social drinking. Working men had to accept being replaced by, or working alongside, women. There were restrictions on the right to strike and other union agreements were suspended. Both working and middle-class men had to pay more of their earnings in taxes. The rich found that petrol for their cars was strictly rationed and, from 1916, so too was food in restaurants.

Yet the war also enlarged men's freedom in the longer term. In 1918, all those over 21 received the right to vote. Trade unions grew in membership and influence during the war years. There was full employment and a better standard of living for poorer workers. In industries like engineering, dilution of skills and more uniform wage rates lessened pre-1914 differences between the skilled and unskilled worker. Many of these changes continued into the post-war period, but full employment was not sustained and, after 1918, workers had to fight to hold on to their wartime gains in living standards.

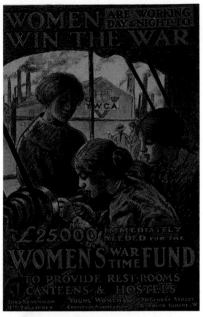

Fig. 9 *Poster illustrating women's industrial contribution to the war effort and some of the changes which this helped bring about*

Cross-reference

The **Defence of the Realm Act**, the **dilution agreements** imposed on the unions and the **extension of the vote** are all outlined on page 40.

Impact on beliefs and attitudes

The war challenged many of society's beliefs and assumptions towards behaviour, morality and religious practice. The stuffier aspects of Victorian society loosened during the war and never quite returned. Education was disrupted because many young teachers volunteered or were conscripted and because large numbers of working-class children left school early, to help meet the need for labour in the economy. About 300,000 children lost their fathers and thousands of children grew up in single-parent households as a result of the war.

The war gave the churches a greater public role. Thousands of chaplains were needed for the armed forces to cater for the spiritual and religious needs of the vast armies. Churchmen were in demand to conduct religious services, preach supportive sermons and carry out burial services. However, the war also provided a challenge to the Christian denominations. Some found it hard to justify the slaughter on the Western Front or to reconcile this with faith in God. A small minority, mainly Quakers, refused to fight and became known as 'conscientious objectors' or 'conchies'. Many pacifists were sentenced to imprisonment; others volunteered for dangerous but non-combatant work at the Front as stretcher-bearers or ambulance drivers.

Some church leaders, including the Pope, tried to reconcile the opposing camps and promote peace. Others preached that the cause the nation was fighting for was just and that God supported it. Church attendance rose a little, having been in decline since the 1850s, but seems to have declined further after the war was over – Rowntree's 1935 survey in York showed that adult church attendance had declined from around 35 per cent in 1901 to less than 18 per cent by 1935. Secular as well as religious beliefs were undermined, especially the belief that progress was both inevitable and beneficial. For four years the supposedly most civilised countries on earth had waged an increasingly barbarous war against each other. This weakened assumptions about the innate superiority of European values and civilisation, and strengthened the ideas of anti-imperialism and anti-colonialism.

Impact on the position of women in society

It is often claimed that the war transformed the position of women. However, it is important to remember that many aspects of social change were already underway before 1914. For example, millions of women had taken jobs, not only in traditional female occupations such as domestic service and in the textiles industry, but also in newer occupations, as typists, telephonists and shop workers. A small number of women were already attending university and entering professions such as medicine and teaching. The war accelerated these changes and helped to loosen traditional social constraints.

Women in the workforce

The war needed women workers – both in larger numbers and in new kinds of work.

Six million men of working age were taken out of the economy into the armed forces and around a million women entered the workforce. A further 250,000 women moved from peacetime to wartime jobs. By 1918, women made up one-third of the total workforce. With reluctant agreement from the trade unions, women took over jobs previously done only or largely by men in factories, offices and transport. In particular, many young working-class women played a crucial role in the munitions industry. By late-1918, around 80 per cent of the workforce in the shell factories was female.

Women replaced men in other sectors of the economy too. In transport, the number of female employees rose from 18,000 in 1914 to 117,000 in 1918. In banking and finance, the number went up by 600 per cent. Thousands of women filled the labour shortage in agriculture. By the end of the war there were women workers even in traditionally all-male industries such as shipbuilding and engineering. Middle-class young women replaced men in administrative jobs and entered nursing, the former having been previously the domain of women from less-affluent families. Women became drivers, secretaries and clerks. Many women also served in the armed forces, to enable men to be freed for frontline duties. Through the Women's Royal Naval Service, the Women's

Fig. 10 *On the buses. Women replacing men in everyday jobs during the First World War*

Auxiliary Army Corps and, later in the war, the Women's Royal Air Force, young women took over a variety of non-combatant jobs. By 1918, some 150,000 women were serving in these auxiliary services as clerks, drivers, wireless operators, mechanics, fitters and so on.

War work brought new working conditions for women. Work in munitions factories, for example, was dirty and dangerous. Many women workers were killed or injured in shell factory explosions. More than 100 died from diseases contracted through handling poisonous chemicals. Women often worked long hours and had to accept shift work, sometimes at night. This disrupted family life and put relationships under strain. On the other hand, war work was also much better paid than domestic service, shop work or even spinning in the textile mills.

> Most of us are up at 5 and the dark winter mornings are cold and comfortless, but thousands of men are out in the trenches, and the constant remembrance of them stifles our groans. Moreover, hardships are not so hard when hundreds of others are sharing it with you. On the whole we are a cheery, friendly team and mighty proud of our work. However, the day is long, the atmosphere is breathed and rebreathed and the oil smells. Our hands are black with warm, thick oozings from the machines. Our hands are not alone in suffering from dirt. Dust clouds filled with unwelcome life find a resting place in our lungs and noses. The enormous wages remarked upon in the newspapers melt somewhat upon inspection. However, there is no doubt that we do earn more than women have ever done before. At the same time living is so expensive in these days.

2

Adapted from Naomi Loughnan's account of munition work in Marlow, J. (ed.),
***The Virago Book of Women and the Great War**, 1998*

Activity

Thinking point

Using Source 2, comment on the way war work affected women's position in society.

Results of the war for women

The efforts of women, at work and in the home, were of vital importance to the success of the war effort and their contribution challenged the dominant Victorian view that women were passive, weak creatures whose only role lay in the home. Many women became the main breadwinner. With full employment and with overtime pay rates, women workers earned more money than ever before. Many young middle-class women often experienced for the first time some degree of financial independence from fathers or husbands. In 1919, the Sex Disqualification Act opened up the Civil Service, local government and jury service to women.

Changes in women's fashions by the end of the war, with shorter skirts and hairstyles symbolised a new freedom for women. Yet, despite this, there were limitations to the social change brought by female wartime employment. There was still a strong emphasis on women's traditional roles, both

Fig. 11 *Women training as fire-fighters to release men for military service*

MANIFESTATIONS DES SUFFRAGETTES A LONDRES
Une sortie de prison triomphale

Fig. 12 *English suffragettes, Edith New and Mary Leigh, being carried triumphantly through London streets after being released from Holloway Prison, 22 August 1908. From 'Le Petit Journal', Paris, 6 September 1908*

during and after the war years. Women were portrayed as responsible for 'keeping the home fires burning', for bringing up the children, and for nursing the wounded. Although employment in domestic service fell by 400,000 during the war, there were still about 1.2 million domestic servants in 1918, almost all of them female and women were still excluded from some key occupations such as coal mining and dock work.

Where women did do the same work as men, they did not always receive the same pay and the increase in women workers was seen as a transitory, emergency measure, rather than a permanent social change. After 1918, many of the women returned either to their pre-war jobs or to their homes. By 1921, the percentage of women in the total workforce was little different from what it had been in 1911.

The Great War and votes for women

One of the key aspects of social change in the First World War is the connection between women's role in the war effort and the achievement of women's suffrage by 1918.

A closer look

Women's suffrage before 1914

In 1897 the National Union of Women's Suffrage Societies (NUWSS or 'Suffragists') was founded by Mrs Millicent Fawcett. Suffragists believed in non-violent methods – petitions to parliament, pamphlets and meetings. The Women's Social and Political Union (WSPU or 'Suffragettes') was formed in Manchester in 1903 by Mrs Emmeline (Emily) Pankhurst and her daughters and believed in direct action – mass demonstrations, hard-hitting posters and the breaking of windows in Downing Street. Suffragettes chained themselves to railings and went on hunger strike when arrested. To avoid the embarrassment of women dying in prison, the government ordered forced feeding in 1909. In 1910–11, parliament proposed a compromise measure, the Conciliation Bill, to give at least some women the vote. Suffragette activity was temporarily suspended but Asquith did not deliver his promises. Between 1912 and 1914, suffragette campaigns became more extreme, with hunger strikes, prompting the government to bring in the 'Cat and Mouse Act' in 1913. Suffragettes burned down buildings, including Lloyd George's house. In 1913, Emily Davison committed suicide at Epsom racecourse. By 1914, the NUWSS had 50,000 members. The WSPU was smaller but made a national impact.

The suffrage campaign certainly put the question of votes for women on the political agenda and convinced a significant number of male politicians and sections of the press that the existing situation was illogical and unfair. However, the violent image of the suffragettes hardened opposition to extending the franchise to women. When war broke out, the suffragette campaign ended and Mrs Pankhurst called on her followers to fully support the war effort.

The women's suffrage campaigns were suspended in wartime as women devoted themselves to the war effort. Such help changed attitudes. In August 1916, J. L. Garvin, editor of *The Observer* wrote: 'Time was when I thought that men alone maintained the State. Now I know that henceforth the modern State must depend on men and women alike.' Even politicians like Asquith who had previously been strongly opposed to the female vote were won round.

Furthermore, the introduction of military conscription for men and the high death and injury rate made it impossible to go on with a system that denied the parliamentary vote to so many men. War had made the need for a wider male vote essential, and naturally this led to a consideration of votes for women. The Representation of the People Act 1918 gave some women the vote at the age of 30, if they were married to a householder. It took until 1928, however, to give all women the vote on the same terms as men – at 21 years.

However, it would be unfair to claim that war alone brought the women's vote. The pre-war expansion of female employment and the suffragist and suffragette campaigns must all have played a part. It is even possible that the war delayed the granting of votes for women. Pre-war Liberal and Labour fears that a property-based franchise for women would unduly benefit the Conservatives was offset in 1918 by extending the vote to all working-class men. Nor did the 1918 Act bring an immediate transformation of politics.

Ironically, most of those women who had flooded into the wartime munitions factories did not get the vote in 1918 because they were too young. Few women were selected as parliamentary candidates; even fewer were elected as MPs. Those who had feared that votes for women would cause 'radicalism' need not have worried. Most women voters turned out to be more conservative and moderate than their menfolk were.

Conclusion

Britain emerged from the war a changed nation. The empire was being challenged by the ideas of colonial independence. The problem of Ireland was still a pressing concern. Britain was weaker economically, facing serious difficulties in paying off debts and rebuilding overseas trade. The war had vastly strengthened Socialism, at home and abroad. Fear of the rise of Socialism had even caused King George V to refuse requests for the royal family of Tsarist Russia to live in exile in England, because of the fears of provoking hostility from the working class. Parts of British society had been shaken out of the pre-war patterns of life. The ascendancy of the Liberal Party since 1906 was over. Whoever governed Britain in the post-war years was in for a challenging time.

Summary question

How far did the First World War change British society?

Cross-reference

More information on the **Representation of the People Act** 1918 is found on pages 35–9.

Exploring the detail

Anti-imperialism in 1919

Britain's Empire seemed to be strengthened by victory in the First World War. Troops from the dominions took part in the fighting, and new colonies were acquired after the collapse of the German and Turkish Empires. On the other hand, the war encouraged ideas of self-determination and hostility to colonial empires, strongly encouraged by the US President Wilson. National independence movements emerged such as in British India. Decolonisation did not happen until after 1945 but the process was already beginning in 1919.

4   Crisis and recovery: Britain 1918–29

Fig. 1 *David Lloyd George, the 'Welsh Wizard' addressing the House of Commons. Lloyd George was a dynamic and charismatic speaker, whose speeches included memorable lines such as 'What is our task? To make Britain a fit country for heroes to live in'*

■ The post-war crisis and the role of David Lloyd George in domestic politics, 1918–23

For the people who lived through the post-war decade in Britain, it was a time of uncertainty and mixed blessings. In many respects, the years from 1918 to 1929 were years of success. Britain had emerged victorious from a major war. Britain was both an empire and a major European power, with great international prestige and diplomatic influence. For many sections of society, the 1920s was a time of prosperity, with rising living standards, new consumer goods and new opportunities in leisure and mass entertainment. There were countless reasons why people in Britain could regard themselves as being fortunate to live in such a stable, modern society, compared with the deep problems that affected many countries in continental Europe.

Beneath the surface, however, lay many economic, political and social problems. Britain had been on the winning side in the First World War but victory came at a terrible cost. The mass casualties left the country with awkward demographic problems, not least the shortage of marriageable men. The demobilisation of millions of men and absorbing them into the peacetime economy proved very difficult. The national economy was crippled by war debts and it was not easy to switch the war economy back to peacetime conditions. International trade had been disrupted, leaving Britain's staple industries with a difficult future. The war had strengthened Socialism and the trade unions – governments in the 1920s constantly had to deal with industrial unrest.

Thus, there were both winners and losers in the Britain of 1918–29, those who benefited from economic prosperity and new opportunities; and those who faced hardship and instability. Unemployment remained stubbornly high throughout the decade, despite all government attempts to improve the situation. There were also winners and losers in politics. Until 1918, the Liberal Party had held a dominant position in Britain's two-party system, while the Labour Party was a relatively new political movement, with limited electoral support. Already by 1918, however, the Liberals were divided and in decline. This decline became steeper and steeper as more Liberal voters shifted towards Labour. In 1923, and again in 1929, Labour governments were formed, though they lasted only briefly. By 1929, it was becoming apparent that Liberal decline was irreversible and that there had been a major realignment of British politics.

The post-war coalition government

Lloyd George, who campaigned on a commitment to work in coalition with the Conservatives under Bonar Law, was re-elected in the 'coupon election' of December 1918. Lloyd George was to be prime minister, even though the Conservatives were by far the biggest single party. Opposition to the new coalition government was weak. The Asquithian Liberals gained only 28 seats. Labour became the main opposition party.

Sinn Fein won 73 seats but refused to participate in Westminster politics. Instead, they established an unofficial Irish 'parliament' – the Dail – in Dublin. The success of Sinn Fein in the 1918 election and the decline of the Irish Nationalists made it clear that the problem of Ireland would have to be urgently addressed – and was bound to be extremely difficult for the new government to resolve.

The new government depended upon Conservative support but had at its head a radical Liberal prime minister, Lloyd George, who had been the bitterest enemy of the Conservatives at the time of the constitutional crisis of 1910–11. Coalition governments in peacetime are rare in British politics but the reasons for this one were rooted in the experiences of the war. The war coalition was regarded as having been both patriotic and effective, reflecting a united nation working together to win the war. It was felt that a government combining the talents of all parties would help restore 'normality'. There was also the hard political reality that, with the Liberals split and Labour refusing to join a coalition, Lloyd George had no choice but to turn to the Conservatives if he was to stay in power.

The Conservatives were still prepared to support Lloyd George because of his sheer standing in the country – 'the man who won the war' – as the press referred to him. His reputation stood so high that the Conservatives felt they would benefit from an alliance with him. They respected his leadership skills, imagination and drive and they knew that Lloyd George's reputation as a social reformer could be very useful in staving off political extremism, of the kind seen in several European countries.

However, Lloyd George was a prime minister in a weak position. His power rested less on his own party supporters than on his former political enemies.

Key chronology

1918 November	The 'coupon election'.
1919	Start of the Anglo-Irish War.
	70,000 on strike in Glasgow, red flag raised.
1919 June	Nationalisation of coal recommended by Sankey Commission.
1919 July	Housing and Town Planning Act.
1920 December	Partition of Ireland.
1921 March	Resignation of Bonar Law.
1921 April	Threat of a general strike.
1921 June	2 million unemployed.
1921 December	Anglo-Irish Treaty; creation of Irish Free State.
1922 February	Geddes Report to the Treasury.
1922 July	Honours Scandal over alleged sale of peerages.
1922 August	Start of Chanak crisis.
1922 October	Carlton Club meeting.
1923 April	Bonar Law appointed prime minister.

Cross-reference

The **Liberal Party split** between the supporters of Lloyd George and the adherents of Asquith and the **coupon election** of 1918 are discussed on pages 36 and 38.

To recap on the **Ulster crisis** and the **Third Home Rule Bill**, see page 30.

The **constitutional crisis** of 1910–11 is detailed on page 27.

■ Activity

Thinking point

Looking at the cartoon in Figure 2, and using the evidence in this chapter, explain what the cartoonist is trying to say about Lloyd George and his political situation at this time. Assess how skillfully his message is put across.

As long as he was successful he could retain Conservative support but, as the wartime spirit receded, it would not take much for the Conservatives to withdraw their backing. Lloyd George had no strong political base of his own. He was leader of one wing of a divided party that was in decline. Lloyd George still had his old radical instincts for social reform and had made promises during the 1918 election campaign, such as 'homes fit for heroes',

PUNCH, OR THE LONDON CHARIVARI.—JANUARY 25, 1922.

THE COLOSSUS: A TALE OF TWO TUBS.

Mr. Lloyd George. "GENTLEMEN, THE IDEAL CONDITIONS ARE THOSE DESCRIBED IN THE HALLOWED WORDS OF THE POET:—

'Then none was for a Party;
Then all were for the State.'

(Aside) L'ÉTAT, C'EST MOI."

Fig. 2 *A difficult balancing act. Lloyd George trying to hold together his post-war coalition. Cartoon from 'Punch', London, 15 January 1922*

but carrying out such policies would not be easy. In the end, the 'coupon election' proved a disaster, both for the Liberal Party and for Lloyd George.

Economic problems facing the Lloyd George government

Lloyd George's government had to cope with some serious difficulties. Some difficulties, such as competition from the rising economic power of Germany and the United States, worries about the growth of the trade union movement and divisions over Home Rule for Ireland, had existed before 1914. Others stemmed directly from the war: government debt; the dislocation of trade and industry; and the problem of demobilising more than 5 million men. Lloyd George had to confront all these issues whilst playing a full part in the long and complex negotiations for the post-war peace settlement but his government enjoyed some initial success.

■ Exploring the detail

Britain and the post-war peace settlement

Along with Wilson of the USA and Clemenceau of France, Lloyd George was one of the three dominating personalities of the Paris Peace Settlement in 1919–20. The peacemakers had to completely redraw the map of Europe and the negotiations were long and complex. Lloyd George faced disagreements with his allies. He thought France was wrong to punish Germany excessively; he was worried that Wilson's idealism would undermine the British Empire. It is symbolic that an unsolved dispute from the peace treaty (between Turkey and Greece) ended Lloyd George's career in 1922.

Fig. 3 *Problems facing Lloyd George and his coalition government*

His coalition contained a number of talented politicians, including A. J. Balfour and Winston Churchill. New ministries for health and transport were set up and Churchill took responsibility for demobilisation, which was carried through in 1919 without making unemployment significantly worse. The economy was switched from war production to peacetime working and controls over prices, rents and profits were ended. Rationing of food gradually disappeared. The railways were returned to private ownership and were reorganised into four companies for greater efficiency, while the coal industry was re-privatised. There was a brief post-war boom although, by the end of 1921, unemployment had reached 2 million. This was largely because of the failure of Britain's **staple industries**. The cotton industry, for example, found it very difficult to win back its pre-war trading position while the coal mines were in serious need of modernisation.

A commission under Lord Sankey looked into the coal industry and recommended **nationalisation** but the Conservatives could not stomach this idea. There was considerable unrest in the coalfields and everywhere trade unions grew stronger and more militant. Membership of trade unions had doubled from approximately 4 million to 8 million between 1914 and 1920 and the early-1920s also saw the creation of very large unions through amalgamation, such as the **Transport and General Workers Union (TGWU)**, led by Ernest Bevin. Industrial unrest brought disruption. In 1919, there was a police strike in Liverpool, and serious riots in Glasgow. In May 1920, dockers refused to load a ship with weapons to be used against the Bolsheviks in the Russian Civil War; and a 'Hands off Russia' campaign got support from the unions. In April 1921, a national miners' strike was sparked off by the owners cutting wage rates. The threat of a general strike led the government to pass the 1921 Emergency Powers Act, which made provision for a 'state of emergency'.

Key terms

Staple industries: the key industries of the British economy on which Britain's wealth rested in the 19th century, such as cotton, coal, iron and steel, shipbuilding and heavy engineering.

Nationalisation: taking an industry into State ownership, organisation and control.

Transport and General Workers Union (TGWU): led by Ernest Bevin, this eventually became the trade union with the largest membership and covered the widest number of types of employment.

Nevertheless, there were some important social reforms including Addison's Housing Act 1919, which led to over 200,000 good quality 'council houses' being built for the working class, and Fisher's Education Act 1918, which raised the school leaving age to 14 and promised part-time education up to 18. Old age pensions were extended, war widows pensions were introduced and a new National Insurance Act extended unemployment benefit to cover an extra 8 million workers earning below the average wage. Such reforms cost money however and, coupled with the problem of repaying war debts, the government was placed under considerable financial pressure. In 1921, Lloyd George appointed Sir Eric Geddes to head a committee examining government spending. Geddes's proposed spending cuts of £86 million most notably in education and public health. Although Lloyd George managed to reduce the cuts to £64 million, the 'Geddes Axe' severely limited the post-war social reforms leaving many working-class voters feeling that the promise of a 'land fit for heroes' had been betrayed.

The problem of Ireland

The government also faced the problem of Ireland. The 1912 Home Rule Bill was due to become law but the divisions in Ireland were intense. The Irish Nationalist Party had been overtaken by the more militant Sinn Fein and many Catholic Irish regarded the men of the 1916 Easter Rising as heroes and martyrs. British rule had been directly challenged by the setting up of the Dail in Dublin and the rise of the Irish Republican Army (IRA). Escalating violence led to the outbreak of the Anglo-Irish War in 1919, a conflict that continued until 1921.

Lloyd George attempted to deal with this using a mixture of repression and reform. The government deployed the 'Black and Tans' (ex-soldiers wearing a uniform that combined army khaki with police dark blue) to fight the IRA. The 'Black and Tans' earned a reputation for ruthlessness but were unable to eliminate the IRA.

In 1920, Lloyd George passed the Government of Ireland Act, partitioning Ireland to preserve Unionist rule in the north and to allow autonomy to the Catholic nationalist south. A Council of Ireland was to be set up to encourage cooperation between the two areas. Partition was aceepted by Ulster unionists and the Province of Northern Ireland was created. It was still a part of the United Kingdom, but had its own parliament at Stormont Castle in Belfast. The Sinn Fein, however, rejected the act, wanting nothing less than complete independence from Britain for the whole of Ireland. The Anglo-Irish War continued until it reached a stalemate in 1921 and Lloyd George proposed a second solution. The Anglo-Irish Treaty proposed that Ireland become a self-governing dominion of the British Empire, known as the Irish Free State.

■ **Cross-reference**

The **earlier developments in Ireland** can be traced through pages 5 and 30–2.

Lloyd George persuaded the Sinn Fein representatives who came to Downing Street to discuss his proposals that, although Ulster might remain separate, it would be so small and unviable that it would soon join the united Ireland. On this basis, Sinn Fein signed, but they opened up deep divisions among the Nationalists.

A powerful minority within Sinn Fein, including the leader Eamon de Valera, rejected the deal and a vicious civil war between the 'pro' and 'anti' treaty factions in Sinn Fein followed until 1922. It ended with victory for de Valera and the murder of his main opponent, Michael Collins. Partition was confirmed and the borders between Ulster and the Irish Free State fixed. The Irish problem at last appeared to be solved, but the leaders of the Irish Free State continued to claim sovereignty over all of Ireland and not until 2007 was an agreement over the permanence of partition finally reached.

Lloyd George has been fiercely criticised for policy failures that led to the Anglo-Irish War, civil war in the south and the emergence of a regime in Northern Ireland that relied on repression and discrimination. Many in the Liberal Party and Labour movement were appalled by the methods of the 'Black and Tans' during the Anglo-Irish War, while Conservatives and Unionists never forgave Lloyd George for separating most of Ireland from the United Kingdom. Whether it might have been possible to achieve more in the circumstances of 1918–23, it is hard to say.

The fall of Lloyd George

The resignation of Bonar Law in May 1921 had weakened Lloyd George's relations with the Conservatives within his coalition but, until 1922, it seemed likely that the coalition might continue beyond the next general election.

However, in 1922, the 'Honours Scandal' broke. Lloyd George was accused of selling peerages to finance his own political party through the 'Lloyd George Fund'. This was bad enough but it was followed by a foreign policy crisis, the '**Chanak Affair**', in which the prime minister was accused of acting high-handedly, ordering British troops into action without consulting his coalition partners.

Conservatives began to feel that they might be better off without Lloyd George. Victory in a by-election at Newport convinced them that they had enough electoral support to break away from his coalition and win power for themselves in the next general election. A meeting of Conservative MPs was held at the Carlton Club in October 1922 and key speeches were made by Baldwin and Bonar Law. Conservatives voted overwhelmingly to fight the next election alone and, within hours of this vote, Lloyd George resigned and the post-war coalition ended.

Key profile

Stanley Baldwin

Baldwin was a moderate, 'one-nation' Conservative, known for his ability to reassure people and to smooth over controversial issues. In 1924, he was one of the first politicians to make effective use of the radio to speak to the nation. Baldwin was prime minister three times – in 1923, from 1924 to 1929 and from 1935 to 1937 – as leader of the Conservative-dominated National government. He is best remembered for staying cool in a crisis, as he did with the General Strike of 1926 and the Abdication Crisis of 1936.

Activity

Thinking point

Use the material in this chapter to prepare speeches either for or against the following view:

'Lloyd George solved the problem of Ireland more effectively than anyone in British politics at that time could have hoped for.'

Key term

Chanak Affair: Lloyd George had been a strong supporter of Greece in the post-war peace settlement but, by 1922, Turkish Nationalists had recovered much territory from Greece and were still advancing. When Turkish forces seemed on the point of capturing Chanak, Lloyd George ordered British forces in the area to stop them, by force if necessary. There was no fighting and the crisis passed over but it damaged Lloyd George's credibility at a vital time.

■ Question

Explain why the Conservatives chose to break with Lloyd George in 1922.

The Prime Minister was described this morning in *The Times* newspaper as a live wire. He was described to me as a dynamic force. He is a dynamic force, and it is from that very fact that our troubles arise. A dynamic force is a very terrible thing. It is owing to this dynamic force, and that remarkable personality, that the Liberal Party, to which he formerly belonged, has been smashed to pieces; and it is my firm conviction that, in time, the same thing will happen to our party.

Stanley Baldwin MP speaking at the Carlton Club meeting

The Conservatives duly won the general election of November 1922. The Lloyd George and Asquithian Liberals won 116 seats between them, fewer than the 142 seats won by Labour, and revealing the extent of the Liberal Party decline. King George V wrote in his diary that he was sure that Lloyd George would be prime minister again one day, but this never happened. Although he remained in politics, and managed temporarily to reunite the Liberal Party in 1926, his career was virtually over.

■ Exploring the detail

Lloyd George's later career

Lloyd George was an 'elder statesman' in the House of Commons until the Second World War, but he never came back into government. Although he put forward some imaginative ideas for stimulating economic recovery in the 1930s, he was not invited to join the National government formed in 1931. Later in the 1930s, his favourable view of Hitler after a visit to Nazi Germany discredited his reputation again. By the time his old colleague Winston Churchill became prime minister in 1940, Lloyd George was too old to serve. He died in 1945.

Our differences will never make me think that he did not render great service to this country, for which the country can never sufficiently thank him.

Bonar Law, the Conservative leader, speaking about Lloyd George at the Carlton Club meeting

When the history of the twentieth century comes to be written it will be seen that the greater part of our fortunes in war and peace were shaped by this one man.

*Winston Churchill, in a speech in 1945. Quoted in Jones, T., **Lloyd George**, 1951*

■ Activity

In light of the comments in Sources 2 and 3 and the other evidence of this chapter, write a newspaper account that might have been published on the occasion of Lloyd George's resignation in 1922, assessing the strengths and weaknesses of his leadership since 1918.

The Conservative and Labour governments, 1923–9

Table 1 *General election results, 1922–9*

Election	Labour	Liberal	Conservative
1922	142	116	345
1923	191	159	258
1924	151	40	419
1929	288	59	260

The fall of Lloyd George meant the return of two-party politics. The stunning decline of the Liberals left the way open for the Labour Party to become the main opposition during a period generally dominated by the Conservatives. Under the leadership of Ramsay MacDonald, Labour actually got into power in 1923–4, and again in 1929, but these were

■ Key chronology

Governments 1918–31

1918–22   The Lloyd George coalition.

1922–3   Conservative.

1923–4   First Labour government.

1924–9   Conservative.

1929–31   Second Labour government.

LLOYD GEORGE – CLASS WAR.

Fig. 4 *Britain's first Labour cabinet, 1924. From right to left seated are Arthur Henderson, J. H. Thomas, J. R. Clynes, Ramsay MacDonald (prime minister), Haldane and Philip Snowden. Sydney Webb is on the left in the back row*

minority governments, dependent on support from other parties and never having a free hand to push through policies. It is fair to say that Labour MPs *felt* they were an opposition party, even when there was a Labour prime minister.

After just eight months in power between 1922 and 1923, the Conservative leader, Bonar Law, who was already very ill, resigned and was succeeded as prime minister by Stanley Baldwin. However, Baldwin's decision to call a general election in December 1923, on the issue of tariff reform, proved disastrous and Ramsay MacDonald became the first-ever Labour prime minister in 1924.

Ramsay MacDonald's government had some success in convincing people that the Labour Party was moderate and could be trusted not to bring in wild socialist policies; but keeping a minority government going by depending on Liberal support was very difficult, even though Labour was helped by the continued split in the Liberal Party. It passed some useful reforms, such as raising old age pensions and unemployment benefit; Wheatley's Housing Act 1924, which resulted in 0.5 million new council houses being built over the next 10 years; and setting up a committee on the future of secondary education. However, it lasted only 10 months because the Liberals withdrew their support and MacDonald could not continue.

The fall of MacDonald's government was closely linked to accusations that Labour was 'soft on Communism'. Part of this was the row over the trade deal with the USSR. Another factor was criticism of MacDonald over his indecisive handling of the so-called Campbell case. Campbell was a communist journalist who had urged men in the armed forces to disobey orders if ever they were sent to put down a general strike. MacDonald's failure to deal effectively with the Campbell case was the

Key term

Minority government: one that is dependent upon the support of another political party to stay in office. In 1924, the first Labour government was brought down when the Liberals refused to continue their support.

Exploring the detail

The growth of Labour

The parliamentary Labour Party grew from 60 MPs in 1918 to 288 in 1929. In the process it overtook the Liberals to become the second main party in British politics. It had gained from the 1914–8 war and from the extension of the franchise to all working men in 1918. In 1918, a new party organisation and constitution were adopted and Labour's electoral success was also aided by the continued split in the Liberal Party. Some Liberal voters switched to Labour which, under Ramsay MacDonald, gained a 'respectable image'.

last straw for his minority government and he resigned. This led to a general election in October 1924, the third in less than two years; and the election campaign was dominated by the issue of Labour's links to communist extremism.

Four days before election day, the *Daily Mail* published the 'Zinoviev Letter', supposedly sent from the leadership of the USSR to the British Communist party to promote acts of subversion in Britain. The Zinoviev Letter was ruthlessly exploited by the Conservatives and damaged Labour's campaign in the vital last days before polling. The scale of Labour's defeat should not be overstated (Labour's share of the total vote went up compared with 1923) but the Conservatives won enough seats for Stanley Baldwin to form a government. The Liberals trailed in third and Baldwin's government remained in power until 1929.

During these years, there was a degree of economic recovery and Baldwin was very successful in projecting an image of calmness and stability despite the underlying economic problems and industrial unrest.

Economic problems, 1923–9

Fig. 5 *Steel works c1925. Iron and steel were amongst the staple industries of the British economy. Several of these were already in decline by the 1920s*

The state of the staple industries that had accounted for almost half Britain's total output, a quarter of employment and three-quarters of exports before 1914 was to be a key problem for most of the inter-war period. As a result, throughout the 1920s unemployment remained at about 10–15 per cent of the insured workforce, although there were considerable regional variations. Britain's share of the world export trade fell, from 18 per cent to 11 per cent and there was also a drop in the value of overseas investments, which left Britain struggling to pay for imports. The city of London was no longer the undisputed financial capital of the world and, as the USA replaced Britain as the world money-lender, the US dollar displaced the pound as the world's major currency.

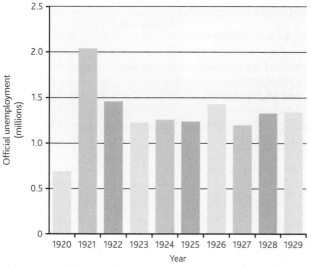

Fig. 6 *Unemployment figures, 1920–9*

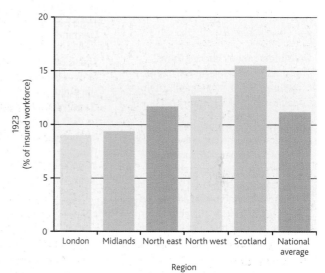

Fig. 7 *Regional unemployment, 1923*

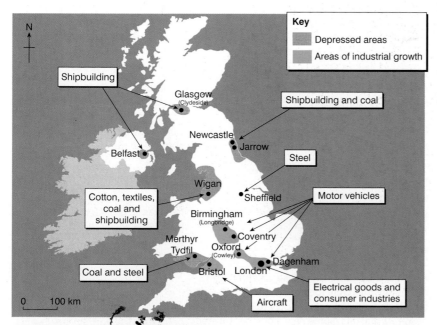

Fig. 8 *Industry in the 1920s and early 1930s*

Did you know?

It is difficult to be exact about figures for unemployment. Before 1911 there were no official statistics, making comparisons with the inter-war period difficult. Even between the wars the official figures, based on national insurance, did not cover everyone seeking work and so underestimate the true total. The figures for those registered as unemployed also fluctuated during the year so the annual figures are an average.

Activity

Source analysis

1. What patterns or trends are revealed in Figures 6, 7 and 8 and Table 2 on page 58? Explain these.

2. What might be the economic and social consequences of these patterns and trends?

Activity

Source analysis

Britain's problems were partly the result of changes in 'demand' and partly because of Britain's own failure to be able to 'supply'.

Examine Table 3. Make a list of the five factors that you regard as having the most effect, in order of importance.

Key terms

Invisibles: money earned from profits on overseas investments. Before 1914 these helped Britain pay for part of its import bill.

Gold Standard: a monetary system under which the currency was tied to gold. International payments were made in gold and the gold standard was supposed to be a self-correcting system that smoothed out fluctuations in the economy. Britain was on the Gold Standard for most of the 19th century until it was suspended during the First World War. Britain returned to the Gold Standard in 1925 but at too high a level. Britain finally left the Gold Standard in 1931.

Structural unemployment: unemployment resulting from changes in the make up of the economy. Cyclical unemployment results from slumps in the trade cycle and is usually short term. Structural unemployment has deeper causes and tends to last longer.

Trade cycle: The economy moves through a cycle of periods of expansion and recession. In periods of expansion demand is high and output, employment and profits follow. The economy grows at a faster rate. When in recession, demand slackens and output, employment and profits reduce. Economic growth slows.

Table 2 *Economic trends, 1913–39*

Year	Coal (millions of tonnes dug out)	Iron (millions of tonnes of pig iron output)	Cotton (millions of metres of cloth exported)
1913	292	10	6,469
1929	261	8	3,443
1938	231	7	1,324

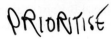

Adapted from Walsh, B., British Social and Economic History, 1997

Table 3 *Causes of the economic problems of the 1920s*

Demand side factors	Supply side factors
The Great War led to lost export markets, and to over-production in industries like steel and shipbuilding. It also disrupted international trade. World trade took until 1925 to return to 1913 levels. The war forced Britain to sell off many overseas investments. Returns from these '**invisibles**' were now reduced. The war also forced Britain off the **Gold Standard**, weakening the pound as a trading currency.	The age and backwardness of the staples pushed up the costs of production. The average British coal mine in 1920 was over 50 years old. Much of the machinery in the textile industry was out dated. Industrial relations in the coal industry were poor, whilst shipbuilding was full of restrictive practices. All these made the staples less competitive.
Foreign competition intensified in the 1920s. British coal faced competition from Poland and Germany; cotton faced competition from India, the USA and Japan. Oil increasingly replaced coal as fuel in ships and some countries began to develop hydro-electricity. There was an excess of coal for most of the 1920s.	Government economic policy sometimes made things worse. The Geddes cuts in 1921 deepened unemployment. In 1925, Britain went back on the Gold Standard at the pre-war rate of exchange – this raised the cost of British exports by 10%. There was also no consistent policy to assist the declining industries to restructure and modernise.
Restrictions on trade also lowered demand. America imposed tariffs on certain imports. Italy tried to move to greater self-sufficiency. Soviet Russia tried to avoid reliance on the capitalist countries. Restrictions on trade and tougher foreign competition hit the staples hard because they were great exporting industries.	Bad industrial relations also hit some of the staple industries, notably coal in the early 1920s. Strikes and disputes especially the General Strike in 1926 meant lost output and markets.
Decline of the staples produced **structural unemployment** in the 1920s especially in the old industrial areas of north and west Britain.	The **trade cycle** produced two major slumps in the 1920s. The first was in 1921–2, the second from 1929 onwards. These cyclical slumps pushed unemployment over 2 million.
A shift in the location of industry. Before 1914 most industries were located near the coalfields but electric power freed industry to locate nearer its markets. Some new industries located in the older industrial areas (such as chemicals near the Mersey and the Tyne) but most favoured the Midlands and south east, thus unemployment in those areas was lower than in the old industrial areas of the north and west.	

There were some positive developments in the British economy in the 1920s. The new industries of the 'Second Industrial Revolution' – chemicals, motor vehicles, electrical goods and canned foods – were growing at a fast pace. Motor car production by the mid-1920s was three times what it had been in 1913. The setting up of the Central Electricity Generating Board in 1926 and the development of the National Grid (a system for transmitting a standard voltage of electricity around the country) brought a new and much more flexible form of power to industry as well as homes. Productivity measured as output per worker also increased. Between 1923 and 1929, overall economic growth was faster than before 1914. The service sector also grew, due to the spread of retailing, road transport, mass entertainment and administration. Generally rising living standards encouraged its continued development. Perhaps as many as a million jobs were created in the service sector during the 1920s.

Fig. 9 *Loading a biplane with passengers and luggage at Croydon Aerodrome, London. Aircraft production and civil aviation were representative of the new manufacturing and service industries developing between the wars*

Cross-reference

For details of the problems facing **Lloyd George's coalition government** 1918–22 and the government's policies in relation to these, see pages 50–2.

Government economic policies, 1923–9

All governments in the 1920s attempted to overcome the structural economic problems that saw Britain lag behind overseas competitors. Table 4 provides a brief overview of some of the main policies and their impact.

Table 4 *Economic policies, 1923–9*

Government	Problem	Attempted solution	Overall assessment across the period
Conservatives 1922–3	Trade	Stanley Baldwin proposed tariff reform to protect British industry from foreign competition.	The Conservatives fought the 1923 election on protectionism but miscalculated and lost power.
Labour 1923–4	Trade	The Labour government signed a trade treaty with Soviet Russia to revive Anglo-Russian trade.	This was cancelled by Baldwin's Conservative government elected in 1924.
		MacDonald helped negotiate the Dawes Plan in 1924 and the Young Plan in 1929. Both aimed to restore Germany as a trading partner by easing the burden of reparations.	The German economy did recover to a large extent, due to American loans and investments. British trade with Germany revived from the mid-1920s.
	Unemployment	The Labour government launched a public works programme, aiming to create jobs by public spending on roads, council houses, etc.	It was on too small a scale and over too short a period to have any great effect.
	Industry	Subsidies were extended to Imperial Airways.	The development of the new industry of civil aviation was encouraged by this decision.
Conservatives 1924–9	Trade	Winston Churchill, Chancellor of the Exchequer in Baldwin's second Conservative government, put Britain back on the Gold Standard in 1925 at the pre-war rate of the pound to gold and other currencies.	Return to gold was welcomed by the banking community. Trade expanded but the exchange rate was set too high, making British exports uncompetitive in staple industries like coal.
		Baldwin's government broke off relations with Soviet Russia.	This stopped the revival of Anglo-Russian trade.

Industrial unrest

Cross-reference

The **Gold Standard** is also covered on page 58.

Economic difficulties brought industrial unrest, particularly in the coal mines where there was a high injury and death rate due to dangerous working conditions. High costs and foreign competition led owners to try to reduce wages, and disputes in the coalfields in 1921, 1925 and 1926 were not about higher wages but about opposing wage cuts. Industrial disputes also took on a political side. Employers and the government feared a socialist revolution in Britain, perhaps led by the newly-formed British Communist Party and backed by Bolshevik Russia, and consequently regarded all union activity with suspicion.

Table 5 *Scale of industrial unrest, 1919–29*

Year	Number of working days lost through disputes in millions	Year	Number of working days lost through disputes in millions
1919	34.9	1925	7.9
1920	26.5	1926	162.2
1921	85.8	1927	1.1
1922	19.8	1928	1.4
1923	10.6	1929	8.3
1924	8.4		

Key chronology

Industrial unrest in the 1920s

1919 Rash of strikes both local and national including a police strike.

1920 Coal miners strike, strike in the London docks.

1921 Coal miners strike.

1925 Threat of a general strike.

1926 April Coal miners locked out.

1926 May General Strike.

The General Strike 1926

In May 1926 much of Britain came to a halt. The coal, iron, steel, chemical and newspaper industries ceased production. In the docks, ships were neither loaded nor unloaded. Railway trains, the London Underground and many bus services stopped running. The government sent soldiers and armoured cars to key places in London. Warships were sent into the rivers Clyde, Tyne and Mersey. World newspapers turned their attention on Britain anticipating the outbreak of violence and revolution. This event, the so-called 'General Strike', lasted nine days in May 1926. Nothing like it had happened before. It aroused controversy at the time and long afterwards.

Even the term 'General Strike' is controversial, for the lead up to the 'General Strike' began not with a strike by the workers but with a lockout by the employers, and although 3 million workers were involved in the General Strike, this was only a fraction of the total workforce. Nevertheless, this 'Great Stoppage' caused bitter differences at the time. To the Conservative prime minister, Stanley Baldwin, it was 'a challenge to parliament and a step on the road to ruin' (*British Gazette*, 6 May 1926). The General Council of the Trade Union Congress, or TUC, however, saw it as being: 'no challenge to the constitution; the TUC is engaged in an industrial dispute' (*British Worker*, 11 May 1926).

The roots of the General Strike lay in the structural problems of the coal industry. Demand for British coal had fallen because of intense foreign competition and the growing use of substitutes such as oil. Many British coal mines were old and inefficient, short of investment. Industrial relations had been bad for a long time and in 1913

Activity

Statistical analysis

Explain the relationship between the statistics shown in Table 5 and those for unemployment in Figure 6 on page 57. What particular events explain the figures for 1921 and 1926? How might the figures for 1927 to 1929 be explained?

Fig. 10 *Armoured car escorting a food convoy through London during the General Strike, May 1926*

The General Strike of 1926

1925 June	Mine owners demand wage cuts and longer hours.
1925 July	Miners appeal to TUC for support, threat of a general strike.
1925 31 July	Government offer to subsidise miners' wages.
1925 September	Commission set up under Sir Herbert Samuel.
1926 March	Samuel Commission reported.
1926 March/April	Negotiations between the unions and mine owners.
1926 30 April	Mine owners' final terms rejected by miners.
	Owners declare a lockout of the miners.
	Majority of trade unions pledge support for the miners.
1926 1 May	Government proclaims a state of emergency.
1926 2 May	Last-minute talks between TUC and Baldwin's cabinet.
	Unofficial strike by *Daily Mail* print workers.
1926 3 May	The General Strike begins.
1926 11 May	Acceptance of Samuel Report by TUC.
1926 12 May	End of the General Strike after TUC calls off support for the miners.

the dockers, miners and railwaymen had formed a 'triple alliance' to support each other in any major dispute with the employers. The miners wanted the coal industry to be nationalised but after the war it had been re-privatised and the owners had tried to combat falling prices by cutting miners' wages. The result was constant disputes, with major strikes and lockouts in 1919, 1920 and again in 1925.

In 1925, the situation in the coal industry was worsened by the government's decision to put Britain back on the Gold Standard at the pre-1914 exchange rate. This made British coal exports more expensive. The owners called for further wage cuts and longer working hours, but the miners rejected these demands, leading the owners to threaten a lockout. When the miners called for support from the railwaymen and dockers, Baldwin's government intervened, offering financial support to subsidise both miners' wages and owners' profits for nine months. It also set up the Samuel Commission to investigate and report on the problems of the coal industry.

The unions saw this as a victory and nicknamed the day the subsidy was announced 'Red Friday'. However, the Samuel Commission Report proved a disappointment. It rejected nationalisation, although it did recommend that in the long term the mines should be restructured with government help and, whilst opposing longer hours, argued that wage cuts were essential to save jobs.

Each side accepted the parts of the Samuel Report they liked, and rejected the rest. When the government subsidies ended in April 1926, the owners declared that from 1 May 1926 the miners would be locked out unless they accepted both wage cuts and longer hours. The miners were defiant, adopting as their slogan: 'Not a penny off the pay, not a second on the day.' The miners appealed to the TUC for support and on 1 May the TUC decided to call on millions of other trade unionists to strike in support of the miners' case.

Encouraged by cabinet ministers such as Churchill, Baldwin failed to take steps to prevent a strike. He could have exerted more pressure on the owners to reach a compromise or shown a greater willingness to talk to the TUC. Instead, he gave the impression that the government wanted a fight with the unions by invoking the 1921 Emergency Powers Act to declare a state of emergency and abruptly ending talks with the TUC leaders after an unofficial strike by printers at the *Daily Mail* the day before the General Strike was due to begin.

The impact of the General Strike

The General Strike lasted nine days and proved a disaster for the miners. The government had the upper hand from the beginning. Under the Emergency Powers Act Baldwin set up the Organisation for the Maintenance of Supplies, which organised 100,000 volunteer workers to supplement the armed forces in moving essential supplies. Through speeches and newspaper articles, Baldwin argued that the General Strike was a threat to the British constitution and he won public sympathy by turning the issue away from the miners' grievances to the question of who ruled Britain – the elected government or the TUC. He did not attack the miners or the TUC directly, but argued that they had been led astray. At the same time, he put Churchill in charge of the government's own newspaper, the *British Gazette*, and let him fight a relentless campaign to undermine support for the strike. The government played on the general desire in the country to avoid violence and disorder. Even the TUC had no wish for a revolution and constantly stressed the need for striking workers to behave well.

Nevertheless, the intransigence of the miners' leaders, Herbert Smith and A. J. Cook, turned public opinion against them. Smith was an uncommunicative Yorkshireman whose answer to most questions was 'Nowt doin', whilst Cook was a Welshman whose fiery speeches frightened the public. This refusal to compromise caused even the TUC to back away from them and it was the TUC that suddenly called the General Strike off unconditionally. The miners continued to fight alone and eventually had to accept the wage cuts and longer working hours demanded by the coal owners.

This climbdown was partly due to failures by the TUC leadership, which had only begun serious preparations a week before the Great Stoppage. No national system for coordinating strike action had been set up and when the TUC called print workers out on strike, friendly as well as hostile newspapers were closed. Although the TUC eventually published their own daily news-sheet, the *British Worker*, it came out too late to make much difference. The TUC was also divided, with moderates like J. H. Thomas, president of the National Union of Railwaymen against the General Strike from the beginning, whilst others like A. J. Cook wanted to use the strike to bring down the government. The TUC had hoped that just the threat of a general strike would be enough to force the government to back down and, when this tactic had failed, was left struggling to find a way out.

Overall, the General Strike did not harm the unions or the Labour Party as much as might have been expected, although in 1927 the government passed the Trades Disputes Act, placing limitations on unions and outlawing 'sympathy' strikes. Nevertheless, Ramsay MacDonald had refused to involve the Labour Party in supporting the strike and had successfully projected an image of firmness and moderation throughout the episode. Even the unions were strengthened in a way. The rows within the TUC about who was to blame for failure in 1926, enabled moderate union leaders like Ernest Bevin to come to the fore. These men did not believe in confrontation and politically-motivated strikes, but in getting a better deal for their members by negotiating with the employers. This image of moderation helped Labour to win the 1929 election.

The end of Baldwin's Conservative government

Stanley Baldwin's reputation is based on his ability to reassure his party and the people that everything was under control. The handling of the miners' strike provided one dramatic example of Baldwin's style of politics. On the other hand, Baldwin hardly had a record of unbroken success. He was leader of the Conservatives for 14 years and was prime minster three times between 1922 and 1937 but there were many failures along the way, not least the self-inflicted defeat in the 1923 election. Baldwin can also be criticised for the adverse economic consequences of putting Britain back on the Gold Standard in 1925.

Baldwin's government did have successes in setting up the BBC, in building new houses, and in a range of reforms in local government, widows' pensions and health that were pushed through by Neville Chamberlain. It was also during Baldwin's time in office that the Equal Franchise Act at last gave women equal voting rights with men in 1928. Despite these achievements, and despite the relative improvement in prosperity and economic stability in the late 1920s, the Conservatives lost power in the 1929 general election.

After their brief spell in government in 1924, Labour had continued its growth at the expense of the Liberals. Ramsay MacDonald had

■ **Exploring the detail**

Baldwin and the *Daily Mail*, May 1926

Printers at the *Daily Mail* refused to go ahead with the printing of an article that they saw as hostile and unfair to the trade unions. The strike was an unofficial one and the TUC quickly persuaded the print workers to return to work. However, by the time they did so Baldwin had gone to bed. This left no time to avoid the start of the General Strike, which was due to begin the next morning – 3 May 1926. Whether this strike was a cause or an excuse remains an open question.

deliberately distanced himself and the party leadership from the wilder activities of the trade union movement and had consequently increased his party's electoral appeal. The Labour Party's programme 'Labour and the Nation' aimed at cautious reform, especially to deal with unemployment, and in the election of May 1929 Labour was rewarded. The party gained new seats in London and the industrial areas. It polled 288 seats as opposed to the Conservatives' 260 and the Liberals' 59, and so became the largest party in the Commons for the first time in its short history. Ramsay MacDonald was invited to form a second Labour government.

Learning outcomes

Through your study of this section you should have a good understanding of the impact of the First World War on British politics and the economy and on British society, and the changes it brought in the role and status of women. Issues relating to the political career and importance of Lloyd George in the years to 1923 have been explored and the ways in which the Lloyd George coalition dealt with post-war problems in the economy and in Ireland have been examined.

Chapters 3 and 4 explored the decline of the Liberal Party and the emergence of Labour as a major force in British politics, and has looked at the ways in which the Conservative and Labour governments of 1923–9 handled economic problems and industrial unrest. You have been particularly directed towards an analysis of the General Strike which helps encapsulate the economic problems of these years. These issues will help you to understand the grave economic problems experienced by Britain in the 1930s which are addressed in the next section.

 Examination-style questions

(a) Explain why a general strike broke out in 1926.   *(12 marks)*

 Explanation of the causes of a specific event almost always means balancing the relative importance of long-term factors as well as short-term ones. You will need to look at least briefly at the industrial unrest in Britain in the early-1920s. But the question asks about why the strike 'broke out in 1926', so you need a direct focus on key events at that time. Remember also to explain, not just to describe in detail what happened.

(b) How important was the decline of Britain's staple industries in explaining the industrial unrest of the period 1918–29?   *(24 marks)*

 The main focus of this question is on industrial unrest – the decline of the staple industries is just one factor among many. If you feel the problems of the staple industries, especially structural unemployment, really were *the* key factor, you will need a lot of evidence about it to back up your argument. However, if you think other factors were more important, then you will be able to write fairly briefly about staple industries and provide depth and detail about those other factors.

MODERATE

5 Economic and political crisis: the second Labour government, 1929–31

BAD LUCK BAD TIMING

In this chapter you will learn about:

- the reasons for the economic crisis of 1929–31

- the political impact of the economic crisis of 1929–31

- the way in which Ramsay MacDonald and the second Labour government dealt with that crisis

- the reasons for MacDonald's resignation and the formation of the National government in August 1931

- the fortunes of the Labour Party from 1931 until its return to government as part of the war coalition in 1940.

> We'll hang Ramsay Mac on a sour apple tree,
> We'll hang Snowden and Thomas to keep him company;
> For that's the place where traitors ought to be.

1 *Anti-MacDonald election song, 1931. Quoted in Pearce, M. and Stewart, G.,* **British Political History**, *2002*

The fate of Ramsay MacDonald is one of the tragic stories of British politics – and a traumatic shock for the Labour Party. The second Labour government started out with high hopes in 1929. Success in the general election seemed to be the culmination of years of growth in support for the Labour movement. The Liberals had become marginalised and Labour was clearly a major player in Britain's two-party system. Ramsay MacDonald was already an experienced political leader, well known and respected, both at home and abroad. Yet within two years Labour would be out of power, smashed to bits in the 1931 election, with less than one-fifth of the seats they had won in 1929. Worse, the party was bitterly split, with MacDonald himself regarded by most of his Labour colleagues as a traitor to everything they stood for.

DEBATE

Part of the reason for this catastrophe was simply bad luck, or at least bad timing. Labour had got into power in 1929 just in time for the Wall Street Crash and the onset of the Great Depression. Part of it was due to personalities and fateful decisions by individuals, especially Ramsay MacDonald himself. However, there was also the special nature of Labour party politics. The 1931 crisis did not on its own cause the bitter party divisions – the pressures of the crisis exposed the deep divisions that were already there.

▣ The policies of Ramsay MacDonald and the second Labour government in dealing with the economic crisis of 1929–31

The second Labour government

When Ramsay MacDonald became prime minister for the second time in 1929, the prospects for his Labour government seemed very favourable. Although Labour was once again dependent on Liberal support for its overall majority in parliament, MacDonald was the election success of 1929 and the opportunity for the Labour Party to put its long-cherished beliefs and ideas into action.

Some important reforms were pushed through in 1929–30. Arthur Greenwood's Housing Act increased subsidies for house-building and introduced new slum clearance schemes. The Land Utilisation Act and Agricultural Marketing Act established a series of marketing boards to help producers. The Coal Mines Act reduced the miners' day from eight

HUBRIS

Fig. 1 *James Ramsay MacDonald, Scottish Labour politician and prime minister in the first two Labour governments, 1924 and 1929–31, at the despatch box addressing the House of Commons*

Key chronology

Labour Party fortunes, 1929–31

1929 May	General election – best inter-war result for Labour.
1929	Second Labour government is formed under J. R. MacDonald.
1929 October	Wall Street Crash and onset of world Depression.
1930 July	Unemployment passes the 2 million mark.
1931 July	Unemployment reaches 2.7 million.
1931 August	May Report and Financial crisis. Labour cabinet divided over government spending cuts.
1931 23 August	MacDonald resigns.
1931 24 August	A National government is formed under J. R. MacDonald.
1931 September	J. R. MacDonald is thrown out of the Labour Party.
1931 October	General election – Labour's worst defeat in its history.

Cross-reference

The economic problems relating to the **decline of Britain's staple industries** are discussed on page 51.

Exploring the detail

The Wall Street Crash

In 1918, the USA was the world's largest economy. At its stock market on Wall Street in New York, millions of stocks and shares were bought and sold daily, their value rising with America's 1920s boom. However, industry could not sustain continuous expansion and, in October 1929, prices began to fall. US businesses went into a downward spiral; imports dropped, unemployment soared and banks closed. Those which had loaned money to Europe recalled their loans and trading levels fell.

to seven and a half hours. Unemployment benefits were increased. On the other hand, several attempts at reform failed through lack of Liberal support. These included an education bill aimed at raising the school leaving age to 15, a bill to create a maximum working week of 48 hours, and plans to repeal the 1927 Trade Union Act.

Much worse than these disappointments, however, was the pressure of outside events. At the very time MacDonald was devising policies to bring about the reduction of unemployment, he and his government found themselves facing a situation that was entirely beyond their control.

The economic crisis

In October 1929, the Wall Street Crash hit the American stock market. The Wall Street Crash did not lead instantly to the Great Depression, which did not reach its worst until 1931, but Britain soon felt the effects of the loss of American markets and the reduction in European trade as other nations also suffered. Between the end of 1929 and 1931, the value of British exports fell by half. Unemployment, already over a million due to the long-term structural decline of the staple industries, rose until it was around 2.5 million by the end of 1931 and almost 3 million by the end of 1932. Industries like coal and shipbuilding were especially affected.

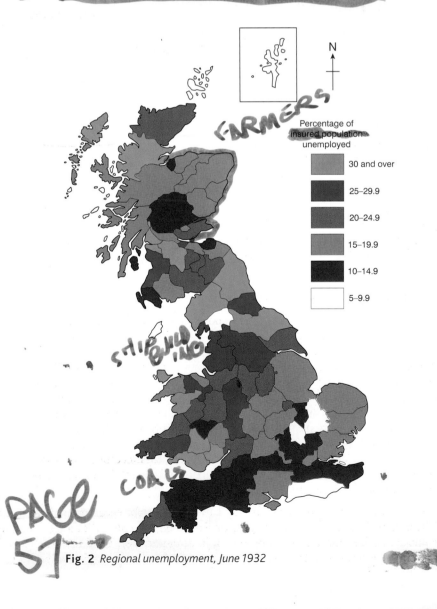

Fig. 2 *Regional unemployment, June 1932*

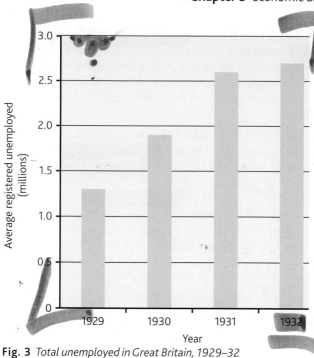

Fig. 3 *Total unemployed in Great Britain, 1929–32*

Statistics taken from Mitchell, B. R. and Deane, P.,
Abstract of British Historical Statistics, 1982

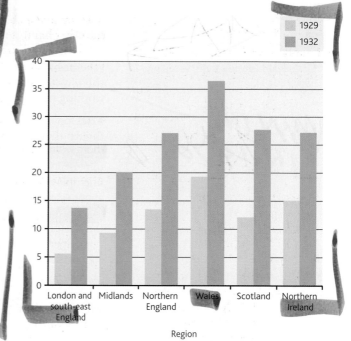

Fig. 4 *Unemployment as a percentage of the* **insured workers** *in each region*

Adapted from Table A11 in Stevenson, J. and Cook, C.,
Britain in the Depression, 1994

Activity

Statistical analysis

Consider the statistics shown in Figures 2, 3 and 4. These are an indicator of the economic crisis of 1929–32.

1. What was the main reason why unemployment was already over 1 million in 1929?

2. What happened to total unemployment between 1929 and 1931?

3. Why would the regional figures have worried governments between 1929 and 1932?

Key term

Insured workers: those workers belonging to the national insurance scheme and therefore entitled to claim unemployment benefit. However, not all workers were in the national insurance scheme in 1930 and so the official unemployment figures do not record them.

Cross-reference

The **concept of balancing the budget** (i.e. not spending more than was earned, a fundamental principle of traditional economic policy) is covered on page 68.

To recap on traditional 19th century economic policies such as **Free Trade, balanced budgets** and the **Gold Standard**, see page 58.

The financial crisis and the Labour Party

The escalating unemployment figures posed a serious dilemma to the new government. MacDonald was no economist and really had little idea of how to tackle unemployment. In 1930, he set up the Economic Advisory Council of industrialists and economists to provide advice, but he remained wary of 'new' ideas. More unemployment meant more unemployment benefits to be paid out and this put a great strain on government finances. Since the Labour Party stood for the welfare of the working man, the provision of benefits was integral to its beliefs. Yet, allowing huge sums of money to disappear in benefits not only undermined MacDonald's traditional belief in a 'balanced budget', it also appeared irresponsible at a time when the party desperately wanted to be viewed as capable and trustworthy.

The Labour Party was divided over how to deal with the economic crisis. The Chancellor of the Exchequer, Philip Snowden, accepted that a balanced budget and maintaining the Gold Standard were fundamental principles. However, balancing the budget at such a time would involve

NAZI 1932

■ **Cross-reference**

Sir Oswald Mosley is discussed on pages 89–91.

MUSSOLINI IN 1920s

public spending cuts which would mean reducing expenditure on welfare. Oswald Mosley, a junior minister, on the other hand, called for an expansionary government spending policy, financing public works schemes and social reforms through government loans. Mosley claimed this was the only way a Labour government should behave – putting working men's needs first.

MacDonald was not convinced that Mosley's ideas would work (even though they were also the views of the brilliant Cambridge economist, J. M. Keynes) – MacDonald was fearful that such radical measures would undermine confidence in the British economy overseas and create even more unemployment. To be fair to MacDonald, even the economists were divided about what should be done. Mosley resigned in May 1930, when his 'Mosley Memorandum' was rejected but, even then, the cabinet could not agree on the size of the cuts needed to balance the budget – and the situation was not helped by the need to win over the opposition party leaders too, whose support was essential for any measure to pass through the Commons.

■ Key profiles

Philip Snowden

Philip Snowden (1864–1937) was a self-educated working man who had risen through the Labour movement to become an MP in 1906. He became Chancellor of the Exchequer in both the first and second Labour governments. Following the collapse of the latter in 1931, he joined with MacDonald in forming the National government where he remained Chancellor of the Exchequer but, in 1932, he resigned in protest at the government's decision to abandon Free Trade.

John Maynard Keynes

While Professor of Economics at Cambridge, Keynes (1883–1946) published *The General Theory of Employment, Interest and Money*, 1936. He believed governments should prevent disruptive slumps and booms by using government spending, interest rates and taxation. Governments should, he argued, spend more than their income in times of slump and pull back in periods of inflation. Keynes' ideas contradicted orthodox economic principles and had little impact in the 1930s. However, they gained support after 1945.

TOO AHEAD OF HIS TIME

RADICAL

Table 1 *Differing views on how to deal with the Depression*

Group	Ideas
Extreme left-wing socialist views	Capitalism was collapsing as Karl Marx had predicted it would. Government should not try to save it but use the collapse to create a socialist economy and society by taking State control and ownership of its main industries, banks and services.
Oswald Mosley's views (similar to those being developed by the economist Maynard Keynes)	The government should borrow money (regardless of increasing debt and unbalancing the budget) and spend more on roads, schools, hospitals and services. This would give the unemployed jobs and spending power and the community better facilities at low cost. Tariffs to protect jobs should be introduced and pensions and benefits increased to boost consumer spending.
Philip Snowden, Chancellor of the Exchequer's 'orthodox' view (shared by most economists, bankers and businessmen of the time)	Keep to traditional economic policies such as Free Trade, balanced budgets and the Gold Standard. Maintain the confidence of international bankers and traders in Britain by cutting government spending to prevent it exceeding income and keep the value of the pound based on gold.

The Wall Street Crash sparked a major European banking crisis in May 1931, which had spread to Britain by July. There was a run on the Bank of England as depositors hurried to withdraw their pounds. As Britain was on the Gold Standard, they withdrew their money in gold, threatening the bank's reserves. The Liberals proposed a committee to consider how the government might curb its expenditure and so restore confidence and MacDonald duly appointed the May Committee, chaired by Sir George May the secretary of the Prudential Insurance Company, to make recommendations.

The May Committee's report was published on 31 July. It came as an unwelcome bombshell to the troubled government. It predicted a massive budget deficit of £120 million by 1932 unless severe cuts were made in government spending. It recommended cuts amounting to £96.5 million with pay cuts for 'public sector' employees, such as teachers, policemen and civil servants and a 20 per cent cut in unemployment benefit and heavier taxation. Interestingly, the two Labour members of the Committee did not agree with these proposals and produced their own 'minority report', but their views were ignored. The report deepened the financial crisis still further by drawing attention to Britain's alleged problems. Nearly a quarter of Britain's gold reserves disappeared and in mid-August ministers, who had set off for their summer holidays just after the report's publication, were recalled for emergency meetings to try to resolve the crisis.

Exploring the detail

The Run on the Bank, 1931

The Bank of England, founded in 1694, held the nation's gold and foreign currency reserves and was responsible for Britain's currency – sterling. In July 1931, foreign investors began to withdraw gold at the rate of £2.5 million a day. On 1 August, the bank borrowed money from French and American banks but the 'run' continued. MacDonald had to return from holiday, in Scotland, to deal with the crisis.

Fig. 5 *Panic on the markets! Bank of England messengers announcing further bad news during the financial crisis of 1931*

Table 2 *Newspaper headlines, August 1931*

	Daily Herald	*Daily Telegraph*	*Daily Express*
19 August 1931	Revenue decision day Cuts in Unemployment Benefit proposed	Economy plans before cabinet Will TUC consent be given?	Bankers, manufacturers, farmers want tariffs now
20 August 1931	Cabinet budget plans completed Salary cuts for teachers, police and others Economies in all government departments		Cabinet's all-day tariff battle Mr Snowden for free trade
21 August 1931	Tories insist on cuts in dole		
22 August 1931	Tariff turned down Mr Baldwin hurries back to London	Grave TUC threat to government Split in socialist party	
24 August 1931	Cabinet on brink of resignation Acute differences over out-of-work pay cuts	National government in prospect Mr MacDonald thwarted by TUC King confers with party leaders	National government expected Government intention to resign

Adapted from Edwards, A. D., **1931: The Fall of the Labour Government**, *1975*

Activity

Thinking point

Study the newspaper headlines on the 1931 financial crisis in Table 2.

1. Use the newspaper headlines to identify the main issues in the financial crisis of August 1931.

2. Which newspapers do you think reflected the views of Labour voters and which those of Conservatives? Explain your answers.

3. What policies were being advocated by the Conservatives?

4. Which policies were being resisted by the trade unions?

5. How do the various newspapers reflect the mood of the country?

The collapse of the Labour government and the formation of the National government, 1931

The fall of Labour

The May recommendations caused an outcry from many Labour Party members and trade unionists. They wanted the government to find money by taxing the rich more heavily rather than by cutting government spending at the expense of the unemployed. Some even believed the crisis could be a good thing – if Capitalism collapsed, then the way would be clear for Socialism. MacDonald, however, felt compelled to follow the broad guidelines of the report. Although he himself favoured taxation increases (and had already raised income tax in 1930), the other parties would not agree to these, and given

IMPORTANT

the importance which he and Snowden attached to a balanced budget and the Gold Standard, MacDonald accepted that a reduction in unemployment benefit was the price his party had to be prepared to pay.

The cabinet was bitterly divided. On 12 August the members of the 'Cabinet Economy Committee', including MacDonald, Henderson, J. H. Thomas and Philip Snowden, met to consider what to do. They agreed to the suggested pay cuts and to a 10 per cent cut in unemployment benefit, which would have taken unemployment insurance back to where it had been before Labour's increase in 1929. However, these cuts of £38 million were substantially less than the May Committee had proposed. By 19 August, the cabinet had agreed to cuts amounting to £56 million – but the leaders of the other parties rejected these as too small. The next day, MacDonald and Snowden met with the TUC leaders, who rejected any cuts at all that would affect the unemployed. They rejected the May Committee's proposals entirely. This put considerable pressure on the Labour cabinet.

TUC

The Bank of England desperately needed to arrange new loans from New York and Paris but the New York bankers would only agree if substantial cuts to unemployment benefits were made. The Conservatives and Liberals accepted this but MacDonald struggled to persuade his Labour colleagues. MacDonald knew that the proposals represented: 'the negation (or abandonment) of everything that the Labour Party stood for' (minutes of the cabinet meeting, 23 August 1931, quoted in L. Butler and H. Jones (eds.) (1994), *Britain in the Twentieth Century, volume I, 1900–1939*, Heinemann) but he argued for a vote of approval in the national interest. On Sunday 23 August, the cabinet gave that vote of approval, but only by 11 to 9 votes. Those who opposed included several leading ministers – Henderson, Clynes and Graham – and the vote split the Labour cabinet so badly that MacDonald could no longer continue to lead it. On 24 August, he went to Buckingham Palace to tender his government's resignation to King George V.

Cross-reference

Arthur Henderson is profiled on page 38 and **Philip Snowden** on page 68.

The establishment of the National government

MacDonald's visit to the King did not have the expected outcome. He had expected to resign but, after the King had spoken to both the other party leaders – the Liberal Herbert Samuel (standing in for Lloyd George who was ill) and Stanley Baldwin for the Conservatives – it was agreed that Ramsay MacDonald would continue as prime minister at the head of a new 'National government' based on support from all the main political parties. At the time, this seems to have been planned to be a temporary arrangement and as a 'government of persons' rather than a full coalition. The Conservatives and Liberals saw certain advantages in allowing MacDonald to continue as prime minister at a time when there had to be drastic economic cuts and generally unpopular measures taken. MacDonald himself may have wanted to remain in office, but he was also persuaded it was his duty to stay on.

The Labour Cabinet was taken completely by surprise. Only three of them – Snowden, Thomas and Sankey – chose to follow MacDonald into the new government. Labour was out but MacDonald was not. He became prime minister of a new National government resting on the support of the Conservatives and some Liberals. Many Labour supporters never got over what they felt was an underhand move by MacDonald and a betrayal of the whole Labour movement. The events of August 1931 led to great bitterness in the Labour Party at the time and to controversy ever since.

Activity

Source analysis

Read Sources 2 and 3.

 1 What do both sources suggest was the reaction of the Labour cabinet to MacDonald's news that he was going to be prime minister of a National government?

2 What does Source 3 suggest was the suspicion that began to grow as Labour supporters absorbed this news?

3 Using the sources and your own knowledge, write a paragraph summarising Labour's reaction to the events of August 1931.

Activity

Revision exercise

You are going to write an appraisal of MacDonald's leadership at the time of the 1931 financial crisis. Start by making your own outline list of ideas, then compare your findings with the comments given on page 73.

Activity

Thinking point

Study Figure 6. How does the cartoonist reveal his own views on the political developments in August 1931? Explain what you understand by the two phrases written on the cartoon.

When ministers met on the Monday MacDonald told them that they were no longer in office. The exception was himself. He would remain Prime Minister, and he would have Baldwin and Samuel as colleagues. When the shattered ministers left, Snowden, Thomas and Lord Sankey stayed behind. I was told that Henderson, MacDonald's most loyal supporter, had to hold on to chair backs to reach the door; he was physically shocked.

2 *Shinwell, E.,* **I've Lived Through It All,** *1973*

At the palace meeting on the Monday morning Mr MacDonald agreed to the formation of a National Government with himself as Prime Minister, without a word of previous consultation with any of his Labour colleagues. He knew he would have the great majority of the Labour Cabinet against him, and practically the whole of the Parliamentary Labour Party. He showed no grief at this regrettable development. I think there are grounds for the suspicion that Mr MacDonald deliberately planned the scheme of a National Government which would allow him to retain the position of Prime Minister.

3 *Adapted from Snowden, P.,* **The Autobiography of Philip Snowden,** *1934*

(Shinwell was a junior minister in MacDonald's second Labour government. Snowden joined the National government somewhat reluctantly but later left it when it abandoned Free Trade.)

Interpretations of MacDonald's action

Fig. 6 *Cartoon justifying the need for a National government, 'Punch', 26 August, 1931*

After the events of 1931, many Labour MPs, party members and trade unionists accused MacDonald of treachery in abandoning the cause of the working man and only thinking of his own career ambitions in accepting leadership of a National government. The later Labour leader, Clement Attlee, said MacDonald's action was 'the greatest betrayal in the political history of this country' and to this day there is a view current among left-wing thinkers that MacDonald gave in to 'Capitalism', and placed the demands of the banking establishment above the deepest held beliefs of the Labour movement.

CAREERIST.

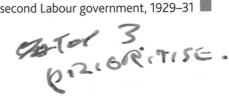

According to his critics, MacDonald was guilty of a long list of 'crimes' in 1931. They claimed that:

■ he had become arrogant and convinced that only he knew best. This made him disloyal to the party.

■ he had needlessly set up the May Committee, instead of relying on the Economic Advisory Council he had set up himself, and had actually allowed Labour's political opponents to decide Labour's financial policy

■ MacDonald was not brave enough to consider new ideas. He had ignored the imaginative schemes put forward by Oswald Mosley.

■ MacDonald was slow to respond to the crisis and so allowed it to get worse. He had allowed the atmosphere of despondency to take hold and to increase the drain on sterling.

■ MacDonald failed to appreciate the depth of feeling within the Labour Party over the unemployment benefit cuts. He was too ready to ignore the unions and the advice of his own cabinet ministers.

■ he sacrificed Labour in the interests of the upper classes. *New Statesman* magazine referred to the 'aristocratic embrace', suggesting that MacDonald had become snobbish and deserted the working class.

■ he had deliberately planned the break up of the minority Labour government in order to forward his ambition to be the 'saviour' of his country

■ when the party split became obvious, MacDonald failed to take the honourable course and resign. He aligned himself with the Conservatives committing the ultimate act of betrayal.

■ he had called an election in 1931, even though he promised not to do so, and the timing of this election caused an electoral disaster for Labour.

For years after 1931, such accusations against MacDonald made him a scapegoat for all the difficulties of the Labour Party – but historians and even a few of MacDonald's former colleagues have put forward arguments in his defence:

■ At the time, MacDonald had no reason to distrust 'orthodox economic principles', which were widely accepted across all parties. It was believed, for example, that coming off the Gold Standard would lead to massive inflation such as had been seen in Germany in 1923.

■ He acted honourably by sacrificing his party principles for the greater national good, under the urging of the King. George V told MacDonald that he had 'put aside all personal and party interests to stand by the country in this grave crisis'.

■ He had continued to borrow money right up to the summer of 1931 in order to maintain the unemployment insurance fund and only changed direction when the Bank of England's gold reserves were threatened. Had he not taken action at this point, confidence in the pound would have been lost with catastrophic results.

■ MacDonald had been one of the founders of the Labour Party and had no reason to want to destroy his own party. What he did, he did reluctantly.

There is no evidence that MacDonald had been planning to become leader of a 'National government' before August 1931 and it was probably not his suggestion even then. According to his biography published in 1977 by David Marquand, the formation of a National government was not what MacDonald really wanted. To him, showing 'responsibility' and acting in the 'national interest' was essential, while those who denounced him thought his primary loyalty should have been to the Labour movement.

Question

Using the ideas given on page 73 and the summary points which you have already made, write an essay answer to the following:

'With reference to the economic crisis of 1929–31, how far does Ramsay MacDonald deserve the title "the Great Betrayer"?'

Key term

Doctor's mandate: means getting support from the voters at a general election for a 'medicine' that might not be pleasant. In this case, MacDonald's National government wanted the public's endorsement for severe cuts in unemployment benefit and public employees pay.

Activity

Statistical analysis

Study the 1931 election results shown in Table 3.

1. Did the National government get its 'Doctor's mandate' from the voters?

2. Who were the real winners in 1931?

3. Explain who the losers were and why.

Cross-reference

Ernest Bevin is profiled on page 52, and is discussed in more detail on pages 102–3.

Ramsay MacDonald was a major figure in the history of the Labour Party, the man who led it through its formative years and headed the first Labour governments. Without the traumatic events and fateful decisions of 1931, he would be remembered as the Great Leader. As it is, his reputation boils down to just one thing – that he was the 'traitor' of 1931. This is not really fair – but, then again, history is not always fair.

■ The 1931 crisis and its impact on the Labour Party to 1940

It is probable that neither MacDonald, who found himself leading a National government dominated by Conservatives, nor Arthur Henderson, who led the bulk of the Labour Party into opposition, fully appreciated the long-term significance of what they did. MacDonald's new cabinet consisted of four Conservatives, two Liberals and three Labour. He had the support of around a dozen Labour backbenchers but he found himself rejected by the rest. A few weeks later, MacDonald was formally expelled from membership of the party. Although Snowden, who became Chancellor of the Exchequer, was able to gain parliamentary approval for the proposed spending cuts – with Conservative support – and the loans which the bank had so desperately wanted were received in September, for all the political upheaval Britain's currency was not saved. On 21 September, the Gold Standard was abandoned. After all this trauma, MacDonald felt the need to call a general election to restore confidence and appeal to the electorate for a '**Doctor's mandate**' for the National government's programme.

This 1931 election was disastrous for Labour as a party, as can be seen in Table 3.

Table 3 *General election results, October 1931*

Supporters of the National government		Opponents of the National government	
Conservatives	473	Labour	52
National Liberals	68	Liberals	4
National Labour	13	Others	5
Total	**554**	**Total**	**61**

From 288 seats in 1929, the Labour Party was reduced to only 52 seats. Among those who lost their seats were many senior figures including Arthur Henderson himself. This crushing defeat provoked further anger towards MacDonald and those who had followed him into the National government. MacDonald himself became the 'prisoner' of the Conservatives while the leadership of the Labour movement passed out of the hands of the parliamentary party, now led by George Lansbury, and into the hands of the trade unions, where Bevin was an important influence.

Key profile

George Lansbury

George Lansbury was a socialist and pacifist. He edited Labour's newspaper, the *Daily Herald* and was also a Labour MP. Between 1929 and 1931, he was Minister for Works in the second Labour government and between 1932 and 1935 he became leader of the Labour Party. Although popular in the party, his uncompromising pacifist views became increasingly criticised as the aggressive aims of Fascist Italy and Nazi Germany became apparent.

Labour recovery during the 1930s

The events of 1931 were disastrous for the Labour Party and seemed to wipe out all the advances made in the previous decade. However, the party did recover in the 1930s, perhaps to a greater extent than was realised at the time. Individual membership figures went up. Labour won most of the by-elections held between 1931 and 1935 and won control of the London County Council in 1934. Although the Conservative-dominated National government decisively won the 1935 general election, Labour gained 154 seats – a gain of 102 seats from 1931. Labour's share of the total votes was 38 per cent, the highest level Labour had ever achieved in any general election, even in 1929. It is worth noting that Labour's total vote in 1931 was actually 30 per cent – the collapse to only 52 seats was more to do with the peculiarities of Britain's 'first past the post system' than with a huge collapse in Labour support.

Fig. 7 *Ramsay MacDonald's National government after the general election of October 1931. Bottom left is Ramsay MacDonald. On the steps in the centre is Stanley Baldwin and on the right with his hands on the rails is Philip Snowden. Neville Chamberlain is second left at the top of the steps*

The gradual Labour recovery continued after 1935. Between 1935 and 1940, Labour won a further 13 by-elections. Because of the Second World War there was no general election again for 10 years, but some historians believe that Labour would have done even better had there been an election in 1939–40, although they probably would not have won power.

Various factors explain the recovery in Labour's political strength, though perhaps the most important factor of all is that it went relatively unnoticed. Most people thought Labour was still lost in the political wilderness when the political facts were different.

Some factors were due to circumstances. There was no serious alternative to Labour as the main opposition party. The Liberal Party had also split over the formation of a National government in 1931, and did so again in 1932 when the government moved away from Free Trade. The 1935 election was a disaster for the Liberals who were no more than a minor party by the end of the decade. Neither the Communist Party nor the British Union of Fascists did well in elections. The Communists won one seat in 1935, the Fascists none and Labour's leaders rejected all attempts to link up with the Communists in a 'Popular Front' against Fascism. This meant Labour's position as the main opposition party was never successfully challenged.

National government policies produced disillusionment among some workers who had not supported Labour in 1931 but went back to Labour in 1935. Under the National government, unemployment rose to almost 3 million in 1932 and high levels of long-term unemployment existed in many parts of Britain throughout the 1930s. Cuts in unemployment benefit, the hated means test and various 'hunger marches' helped to maintain working-class loyalty to Labour.

Exploring the detail

The first past the post system

British elections are decided by who wins the most constituencies. It does not matter if you win by 40,000 votes or by 2. This means that *where* votes are cast matters more than *how many*. Traditional Labour strongholds like South Wales and the north east voted solidly Labour, but this meant that thousands of votes were 'wasted' on winning a few seats by huge majorities. This factor explains why there is often a difference between the total votes cast and the number of seats won.

Cross-reference

The **National government's economic policies**, including the '**means test**', are discussed in more detail on pages 81–2.

Fig. 8 *Clement Attlee (1883–1967). Member of parliament for Limehouse. Leader of the Labour Party 1935–55, deputy prime minister in wartime cabinet under Churchill, prime minister 1945–51*

■ Key terms

League of Nations: set up after the First World War as an international organisation to avoid future wars by settling disputes through negotiation. The rise of aggressive governments in Japan, Italy and Germany threatened its work in the 1930s partly because it had no armed forces of its own. Although Labour had favoured international disarmament, it wanted the League to be effective.

Appeasement: the name of the foreign policy pursued by Baldwin and Chamberlain between 1935 and 1939 in dealing with Fascist Italy and Nazi Germany. Although it was later denounced as a failed and cowardly policy, it was a genuine attempt to settle issues by concession and compromise rather than by war.

■ Activity

Revision exercise

Construct a spider diagram to illustrate the factors aiding Labour's recovery in the 1930s.

There were also ways in which the Labour Party took positive steps to foster recovery. Reforms in party organisation put more influence into the hands of moderate trade union leaders such as Ernest Bevin. Changes in leadership also helped. The seniority and moral standing of Arthur Henderson and George Lansbury were helpful in stabilising the party immediately after 1931, but Lansbury was replaced as leader by Clement Attlee in 1935. Although Attlee lacked charisma, his quiet efficiency and determination enabled him to rebuild the party. A membership drive proved successful and policies were more clearly thought out. In 1934, Labour published its most thorough programme since 1928 and after 1935 it slowly moved away from pacifism, firstly in favour of armed support for the **League of Nations** and by 1939 to full resistance to Nazi Germany. Partly as a result, Labour began to get more support in the press. The *Daily Mirror* became pro-Labour in 1938 whilst the Labour *Daily Herald* became almost as popular as the Conservative *Daily Express*.

■ Key profile

Clement Attlee

Clement Attlee (1883–1967), an officer in the First World War, became a Labour MP in 1922. He held office in the second Labour government but broke with MacDonald in 1931. Following the removal of Lansbury, Attlee became the leader of the Labour Party in 1935. In May 1940, he joined Churchill's war cabinet, becoming deputy prime minister. In 1945, Attlee's party won a landslide victory and he headed two Labour governments between 1945 and 1951. Modest and uncharismatic in appearance he was an efficient leader and after 1945 presided over one of the great reforming governments of the 20th century.

One key factor in the Labour Party in the 1930s was its firm commitment to moderate, 'respectable' policies. There was no lurch to the left. It might seem surprising that the Labour Party did not evolve as a more radical party after the split of 1931. After all, the moderates who followed MacDonald had been in the minority then and many had called for a more anti-capitalist stance and the advance of true 'Socialism' to combat the alleged failures of capitalist society. Elements of the Labour movement expressed their admiration for the socialist society they thought was being constructed in Stalin's Russia. A breakaway movement, the Socialist League, was formed. Sir Stafford Cripps was regarded as the 'champion of the left'.

The vast majority of the Labour movement remained committed to moderation and parliamentary democracy. Attlee's leadership contributed to this, so did the influence of the unions, who played a big part in the 'National Council of Labour' set up in 1934. Ernest Bevin, the boss of the Transport Workers' Union, was fiercely anti-communist and did a lot to prevent the growth of communist influence. The Socialist League eventually dissolved itself in 1937. Sir Stafford Cripps was expelled from the party in 1939 after he tried to organise a broad alliance – including socialists, communists and disgruntled Conservatives and Liberals – in opposition to Chamberlain's **Appeasement** policies. Mainstream Labour opinion refused to countenance any deal which involved communists and did all it could to avoid the taint of 'radicalism'.

The party used the years in opposition to clarify its ideas and to develop a coherent policy programme. The Labour leadership accepted J. M. Keynes' ideas about the need for government to manage the economy. In 1937, 'Labour's Immediate Programme' set out a plan for the nationalisation of British industries.

However, despite this improvement, Labour remained out of government in the 1930s and the Conservative-dominated National government continued to have a large overall majority. Labour's support strengthened in London and in areas in the north of England and Scotland where there had been only limited recovery from the Depression. It did less well in the more prosperous areas and amongst the middle class. Recovery was therefore limited and largely consisted of winning back lost seats and votes rather than power. By 1940, Labour was ready for government, but it had to wait for the experience of war to affect the electorate sufficiently to persuade it that a Labour government was worth electing.

■ Summary questions

1. Explain why there was an economic and financial crisis in Britain in 1931.
2. How far had Labour recovered by 1940 from the trauma of 1931?

■ Cross-reference

After the Second World War **Sir Stafford Cripps** took a leading role in Attlee's government and its austerity policies – his nickname became 'Austerity Cripps'. See page 126.

■ Exploring the detail

Conservative domination

From 1931–45, the Conservatives were the largest party in the Commons. MacDonald lost his seat in 1935 and Stanley Baldwin, the Conservative leader, became the National government prime minister. Baldwin dealt successfully with the Abdication Crisis in 1936, when the new king, Edward VIII, abdicated the throne in order to marry an American divorcee, Mrs Wallis Simpson. Baldwin was then succeeded by Neville Chamberlain in 1937. Baldwin and Chamberlain seemed 'safe pairs of hands', and benefited from a fall in unemployment and some economic revival in the south. With the wartime crisis of May 1940, the National government was replaced by a coalition led by the Conservative Winston Churchill.

6 The National government: economic crisis and political extremism

In this chapter you will learn about:

- the economic problems facing Britain in the 1930s

- the ways in which the National government from 1931 tackled these economic problems

- the emergence of political extremism in the later 1930s

- the limitation of political extremism through the policies of the National government and other factors.

They lounge at the corners of the street
And greet friends with a shrug of shoulder
And turn their empty pockets out,
The cynical gestures of the poor.

Now they've no work, like better men
Who sit at desks and take much pay
They sleep long nights and rise at ten
To watch the hours that drain away.

1

'Unemployed' by Stephen Spender

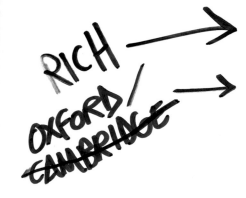

Fig. 1 *Advertisement for Morris cars – one of the growth companies of the 1930s*

The 1930s have been called the black years, the 'devil's decade'. The popular image of the Thirties can be summed up in two short phrases: mass unemployment and appeasement. Yet at the same time, most English people were enjoying a richer life than any previously known in history – longer holidays, shorter working hours, higher real wages. They had the motor car, cinemas, radio sets, electrical appliances. The two sides of life did not join up.

2   Taylor, A. J. P, *English History 1914–1945*, Penguin 1970

[Handwritten margin notes: REGIONALISM; 60s HISTORIAN; LABOUR PARTYS 1945 MANIFESTO TITLE]

Assessing the state of Britain in the 1930s remains complicated and difficult. One reason for this is the way the 1930s came to be regarded during and after the Second World War. From 1940, people looked back at the 1930s as an awful warning, telling themselves 'never again'. The decade was seen in retrospect as a time of economic depression and guilty memories – guilty because of the shame of appeasing Hitler; guilty because of the failure to overcome social divisions, or to protect significant sections of society from the evils of mass unemployment. When Labour won its stunning election victory in 1945, memories of the 1930s were at the forefront of many voters' minds. But these memories did not necessarily reflect the way people felt at the time.

After 1940, for example, most people in Britain had no doubts about the 'guilty men' who had appeased the dictators. Neville Chamberlain in particular was discredited, while Winston Churchill was seen to have been completely vindicated by the national determination that led Britain to victory. Yet, in the 1930s, Chamberlain was hugely popular, at least up to March 1939. Churchill was almost a lone voice on the fringes of politics. Again, later memories of the 1930s did not give an accurate picture of the public mood at the time.

The second problem is that the experience of life in Britain during the Great Depression was wildly different according to where you lived, what class you belonged to, and whether you had a job. Where there was a concentration of older staple industries, working people were hit hard by the Depression, with half the population out of work for years and the collapse of the local economy that had depended on the now closed factories. Where the new industries were expanding, life was very different – a time of affluence, of new suburban houses, new consumer goods, and new opportunities for entertainment and leisure. Britain looked like two nations.

For some, therefore, the 1930s were indeed the time of the great slump, a time symbolised by poverty and life on the dole, with the National government standing idly by and letting the misery continue. For others, it was an age of affluence, with the National government deserving credit for ensuring a degree of economic recovery and maintaining political and social stability.

The National government had the responsibility of guiding Britain through the world Depression and its damaging effects on Britain. There was the nightmare of mass unemployment; there were serious dangers from political extremism, both from the communist left and from the fascist right. Outside Britain there was the rise of aggressive dictators like Hitler, Mussolini and Franco in Spain. How well the National government carried through its responsibilities is a matter of debate. Many contemporaries and many later historians attacked the National government for being ineffectual and doing too little too late. Deciding between these

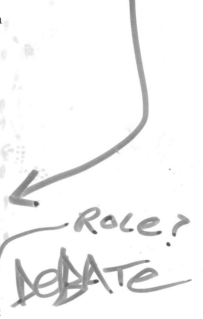

[Handwritten margin notes: ROLE? DEBATE]

■ **Cross-reference**

Labour's victory in the 1945 election is covered on pages 121–4.

■ Key chronology

Governments and the economy in the 1930s

1931 August National government set up and led by Ramsay MacDonald.

1931 September Snowden's budget Britain leaves the Gold Standard.

1931 October General election, the first National government under MacDonald wins huge majority.

1932 March Import Duties Act.

1933 January Unemployment peaks at 2.98 million.

1934 Special Areas Act.

1935 General election – second National government wins huge majority under Baldwin.

1937 Neville Chamberlain replaces Baldwin as prime minister of the National government.

1938 Rearmament programme stepped up.

■ Cross-reference

The **economic problems of the 1920s**, including the **Wall Street Crash**, are discussed on page 66.

■ Key term

Unemployment: unemployment can occur for many reasons. Cyclical unemployment is caused by periodic slumps. Structural unemployment is caused by the long-term decline of certain industries. In the 1930s, Britain suffered from both. Long-term unemployment is usually defined as lasting continuously for a year or more. In the most depressed industries and regions, in the 1920s and 1930s, many were unemployed for years on end.

interpretations is far from easy – but it is the task of historians to look at the evidence and to try to separate reality from the myths.

■ The National government and economic recovery

From 1931 until 1940, Britain was governed by a national government that was not actually genuinely national. Although the ex-Labour leader, Ramsay MacDonald, was prime minister, the National government was not a true coalition of all the parties. The bulk of what was left of the Labour Party was in bitter opposition. The Liberals made not much more than a token contribution. The power base of the National government was the massive majority the Conservatives held in parliament. When MacDonald finally resigned in 1935 and Stanley Baldwin became prime minister for the third time, this Conservative domination became even more obvious.

Economic problems in the 1930s

The impact of the Wall Street Crash and the Depression that followed intensified the existing economic problems carried over from the 1920s, especially the decline of the staple industries. From 1930, world trade shrank and with it the demand for British exports, which fell by a third in volume and by a half in value by 1932. Exports did not fully recover until after 1937. Cotton exports were particularly badly hit. Total output was already falling by 1930; by 1932 it was less than half the 1913 figure. Coal output was 238 million tonnes, by 1933 it had declined to 208 million tonnes. Shipbuilding launched a million tonnes of new shipping each year in the 1920s but produced only 133,000 tonnes in 1933.

As a result, unemployment in these industries rose to frightening levels. In June 1932, over 47 per cent of steel workers were unemployed, twice the average for industry in general. In shipbuilding 60 per cent of insured workers were unemployed in 1932. Moreover, unemployment remained high in these industries for the rest of the 1930s. In 1938, a fifth of coal miners were unemployed and a quarter of cotton workers.

Areas of Britain highly dependent on such industries suffered high long-term **unemployment**. In 1932, over a third of insured workers in Wales and over a quarter in northern England, Scotland and Northern Ireland were unemployed. Towns entirely dependent on one declining industry suffered most. In 1934, Merthyr Tydfil in South Wales had 62 per cent male unemployment, Maryport in Cumberland over 50 per cent and Jarrow in the north east had around 70 per cent. Jarrow, in fact, was the town that came to symbolise the problems of industrial decline and the plight of the unemployed, because of the Jarrow March in 1936, when 200 unemployed men from the South Tyneside shipbuilding town marched 300 miles to London to petition parliament in the hope of government intervention to save the town and its workforce.

The case of Jarrow was only one sign of the way unemployment black spots persisted despite government policies to relieve the situation. In 1937, nearly 30 per cent of the jobless had been out of work continuously for at least one year. In South Wales the unemployment rate was still more than one worker in five. The national figure was still 1.5 million, 10 per cent of the workforce. It was not until 1941, the second year of the war, that unemployment finally fell below 1 million.

A closer look

The Jarrow Crusade

The Jarrow Crusade in October 1936 was one of most symbolic events of the 1930s. Two hundred unemployed men from the South Tyneside shipbuilding town of Jarrow marched 300 miles to London to petition parliament to bring work back to their town. Organised by Jarrow's Labour MP, Ellen Wilkinson, and by the mayor and council, it was supported by the local churches, trade unions and politicians. The orderly conduct of the marchers, the scale of unemployment in Jarrow and the obvious misery that this was causing, caught the public's imagination and sympathy.

Jarrow was a classic example of an industrial town highly dependent upon one of the declining staple industries. Palmer's Shipyard had been the last large employer in Jarrow and when it closed in 1935 male unemployment in the town rose to 77 per cent of the workforce. With no alternative employment, Jarrow was threatened with terminal decline. Attempts to set up a steel works failed due to lack of government support.

Fig. 2 *The Jarrow Crusade, October 1936. Marchers on their way to petition parliament and government for help*

When the marchers got to London they tried to hand their petition to the prime minister, Stanley Baldwin, but he refused to meet them. The mayor was able to address a large group of MPs but the Crusade brought little immediate benefit. The marchers returned and some found their unemployment benefit stopped for not being available for work.

Nevertheless, the March had some results. It raised awareness of the plight of Jarrow and other depressed towns. It led a businessman, John Jarvis, to establish a metal foundry in Jarrow and by 1938 a tube mill, shipbreaking yard and an engineering works brought more jobs. However, it was not until the war brought increased demand for ships that Jarrow's unemployment finally disappeared.

Economic policies of the National government

From 1931, the National government introduced a range of economic policies to deal with the crisis it had inherited. These policies addressed financial problems, trade and industry. Some of these policies were orthodox ones, following traditional principles. Others were more innovative. Historians still disagree as to whether these policies were effective, or if there were enough of them.

In financial policy, the National government:

- aimed to balance the budget and limit government spending to match government income

- made a 10 per cent cut in unemployment benefit and introduced a 'means test'

Activity

Talking point

What does Figure 2 suggest about the 1930s?

Activity

Revision exercise

Imagine you are one of the Jarrow marchers. Write a petition to the prime minister protesting at the situation and asking for something to be done.

Cross-reference

To recap on **orthodox economic policies**, see page 68.

Key term

Means test: was introduced in 1931. The unemployed who had exhausted their insurance benefits could apply for an additional 'dole', but were subject to a means test which took into account the income of other family members.

Good for House Buying →

- implemented cuts in wages of public employees
- aimed to keep the value of the pound stable by intervening in currency markets
- lowered interest rates to 2 per cent in 1932, making 'cheap money' available to borrowers.

In its trade policies, the National government:

- set up the 'sterling area' with members using the pound rather than gold to settle their trading accounts
- passed the Import Duties Act 1932, imposing tariffs to protect British industry and agriculture with exemptions for empire counties
- agreed a form of imperial tariff system at the Ottawa Conference in 1932
- made trade treaties with various countries, allowing a quota for their imports into Britain in return for a similar quota for British exports.

In its policies for industry, the government:

- provided government aid to the most depressed areas through the Special Areas Act of 1934
- passed the Cotton Industry (Reorganisation) Act 1936 to close down non-profitable mills and so reduce surplus capacity in the industry
- passed the British Shipping (Assistance) Act 1935 to provide government loans for shipping companies to scrap older ships and build new ones
- passed the North Atlantic Shipping Act 1934 to provide loans to help restart the building of the huge transatlantic liner *Queen Mary*
- set up marketing boards for milk, bacon and potatoes, providing guaranteed prices for farmers
- provided government subsidies for livestock farmers and sugar beet growers.

How effective were the National government's economic policies?

At the 1935 election the National government claimed in its manifesto that 'Under this leadership we have emerged from the depths of depression to a condition of steadily returning prosperity'. Some National government policies did help reduce unemployment and encourage economic recovery, but others were of limited value.

Cutting government spending in 1931, including the wages of public employees like teachers and policemen as well as unemployment benefit, helped to maintain international confidence and stopped the banking crisis. However, it also lowered total demand for goods and services in the depth of a world depression. Partly as a result, unemployment rose sharply in 1932–3. The 1931 cuts did not save the Gold Standard either. It was abandoned in September 1931, even though one of the main reasons why the National government had been formed was to protect Britain's finances and keep to the Gold Standard.

Leaving the Gold Standard allowed the pound to fall in value, which made British exports cheaper and so helped ease the impact of the Depression. However, its effectiveness was limited because other currencies also left the Gold Standard and they depreciated in value too. Many countries introduced protective tariffs, which made exporting difficult. Britain sold more exports to the empire, within the 'sterling area', but this only partly made up for the decline in demand from America and Germany.

"CHOSE 1" ↗
"FINANCE
TRADE
INDUST.
POLICIES.

A more important benefit of coming off the Gold Standard was that the Bank of England was able to lower interest rates. 'Cheap money' helped recovery in several ways. It made it easier for industries to borrow money to invest in modern machinery and plant. It also made it easier for consumers to borrow money on mortgages to buy new houses. The result was a private house-building boom with 2 million homes built in the 1930s. Not only did house building provide work, it also created demand for furniture and fittings. However, these houses were built mainly for the middle classes who were more likely to have steady jobs and so could take advantage of cheap mortgages and low prices. These houses were mostly built by the private sector. There was much less local government house building; perhaps 700,000 council houses were built in total between 1931 and 1940.

[handwritten notes: LIMITED REGIONALLY. ANSCILLARY JOBS. WK DON'T BEN.]

The Special Areas Act provided only £2 million of aid, and only to the most depressed areas, like West Cumberland. Despite high levels of unemployment, many of the old industrial areas did not qualify. Nor did the National government have much of a regional policy. It preferred the unemployed to move rather than encourage new industry to locate in the depressed regions. Government public works programmes to create jobs were on a much smaller scale in Britain than in America or Germany.

Fig. 3 *One of the many new private housing estates built in the 1930s*

Government schemes to close down uncompetitive shipyards, mills and mines did mean that those that survived were able to attract new investment. In the coal mines, for example, the 1930s saw far more modern machinery being installed. However, although the survivors were more competitive, they employed far fewer workers. In places like Jarrow such closures had a devastating effect on the town, pushing unemployment above 70 per cent. In agriculture, marketing boards provided some security for milk and potato farmers, but less help was given to arable farmers.

Activity

Talking point

1 What does Figure 3 suggest about the 1930s?

2 Compare Figure 3 to Figure 2. What does this suggest about photographs as historical evidence?

3 Which factors in Britain's economic recovery does Figure 3 illustrate?

Activity

Revision activity *H/W.*

Complete the following table, summarising and assessing the National government's economic policies:

Policy	Benefits	Limitations	Effectiveness
Balancing the budget, i.e. balancing government spending with income	Helped maintain international confidence and eased the financial crisis	Reduced overall demand at home	Deepened the Depression further and pushed up unemployment

REG.

Mcc.

REARMOMENT WAIT + CONSUMPTION

Economic recovery

Despite the limitations of the government's schemes in the 1930s, Britain's economy did begin to recover from the worst of the Depression. This recovery was limited and was more obvious in the Midlands and south east where most of the new growth industries were situated rather than in the older industrial areas of the north and west. Total unemployment fell by half between 1933 and 1940 and average economic growth rates in the 1930s were higher than in the 1920s.

New industries such as motor vehicles, chemicals and aircraft enjoyed particular growth. Output of motor cars doubled between 1929 and 1939, making Britain the second largest car maker in the world. Even the staple industries began to recover. Coal production in 1938 was 227 million tonnes, almost back to what it had been in 1928. By 1938, the steel industry was producing more steel than in 1928.

According to A. J. P. Taylor, 'increased consumption by individuals pulled England out of the slump' (Taylor, A. J. P. (1975) *Britain 1914–1945*, Penguin) – in other words, the people spent themselves out of the Depression. Several factors caused this growth in consumption. The Depression itself helped by lowering prices which tended to stay low. This meant that those lucky enough to be in a steady job found that their wages stretched further. This rise in **real wages** helped demand to rise at home and partly offset the fall in demand abroad. Although unemployment was high, there were always more people in work than out of work and this, together with lower prices and cheaper borrowing, created rising consumer demand in areas like house building. General social trends such as the trend towards a smaller family size also meant that those in work had more to spend.

Rising consumer demand led to an expansion of the Home Market, which helped offset cuts in government spending. This stopped the Depression getting worse and helped recovery. Most growth occurred in industries serving the Home Market. For example, the consumption of electricity doubled in the 1930s and the demand for 'consumer durables' such as radios and motor cars grew. By 1938, there were 9 million wireless sets in private homes and 2 million private cars on the road. The Home Market also encouraged the growth of jobs in service industries such as retailing, transport and banking. Numbers employed in retailing and transport rose every year in the 1930s. Mass entertainment was another growing sector of employment with cinemas and dance halls open in almost every town by the end of the decade.

New methods of production such as the assembly line and the use of electric power enabled many goods to be sold more cheaply. For example, the price of motor cars and wireless sets fell during the 1930s and so more people could afford to buy them. A small family car in 1922 cost £220, by 1932 it cost £120. This stimulated growth in these industries. For example, in 1932, almost half of households had bought a radio, by 1939 almost three-quarters had.

The new industries such as motor cars, electrical goods, chemicals and aircraft were less affected by the world Depression than were the old staples. These industries continued to grow throughout the 1930s. The output of motor cars doubled between 1929 and 1939 and the output of electricity quadrupled between 1925 and 1939. Numbers employed in these industries rose as a result. By 1939, the motor industry employed 400,000 workers. However, it was unfortunate that these new industries did not expand fast enough to absorb all the workers shed by the declining staples and that they tended to locate in the Midlands and south east rather than in the old industrial regions.

Key term

Real wages: the term for measuring income by what it will buy, taking prices into account. The best measure of real wages is the number of hours a worker has to put in to be able to buy products.

Cross-reference

To review what is meant by the '**old staples**', see page 51.

Activity

Revision exercise

Construct a summary diagram listing the factors contributing to Britain's economic recovery. For each factor, list (i) the ways in which it assisted recovery, and (ii) its limitations.

REG.

One way government actions indirectly assisted economic recovery was rearmament. Spending on rearmament was increased from 1935 onwards and shot up sharply in 1938–9. Despite the fact that it was forced on the National government by fear of war with Germany, rearmament did what previous policies had failed to do. It directly stimulated both old staple industries like shipbuilding and steel, as well as new industries such as aircraft and chemicals. Rearmament breathed new life into some of the most depressed regions. For example, many of the unemployed of Jarrow found work in 1938–9 either in the new steelworks established in their town or in shipyards on the Tyne meeting orders from the Royal Navy. It was the gradual world recovery from the Depression and the spur of war which helped cure the worst of Britain's economic troubles.

Fig. 4 *New architecture for new industry. The Hoover building at night. The clean lines of the 1930s Art Deco exterior advertise the modern, hygienic appliances produced inside. Significantly it was situated on Western Avenue. Most of the new factories built in the 1930s were located in Greater London*

A closer look

The new consumerism – an age of affluence?

The 1930s is commonly associated with the 'have-nots', the millions struggling to cope with the hardships and the loss of dignity in life on the dole; but life was very different for the 'haves'. For some, especially in the growing middle class, the 1930s was an age of affluence, fuelled by the easy availability of motor cars, smart new fashions, household appliances and lots of opportunities for entertainment, sport and holidays.

The cutting edge of middle-class prosperity was home ownership. Spacious new homes in the new suburbs were being built in great numbers and the availability of 'cheap money' made mortgages accessible to many people who could not have afforded one before. Suburban homes also helped the sales of motor cars, another luxury brought within reach by stable prices and cheap money. Electricity made many new household appliances practical and desirable.

The new affluence was very visible. It was symbolised by the rush of handsome factory buildings, like the Art Deco Hoover factory in Ealing, West London, and by the rapid development of the advertising industry, glamorising the new consumer goods. The new affluence was also divisive. Life in the suburbs had little connection with working-class society. When it did, the reactions were often hostile – in one north London suburb, a high brick wall was constructed to block the end of the road and keep 'the others' out of sight and out of mind. The two nations remained separate.

Activity

Talking point

'Bad times' or 'Good times'? Which best describes the British experience of the 1930s?

Key chronology

Political extremism

1920 **August**	Formation of the Communist Party of Great Britain.
1932 **October**	Formation of the British Union of Fascists (BUF).
1934 June	BUF meeting at Olympia, London.
1936 **October**	The 'Battle' of Cable Street.
1936 **December**	The Public Order Act
1940 May	Arrest of BUF leaders under the defence regulations.

A closer look

The European dictators

The 1930s was the decade of totalitarian dictatorships in Europe. Totalitarianism is a useful label, covering dictatorships of the Left, or the Right – and the mixture of the two that went to make up fascist ideology. Totalitarian regimes depended on the police state and the use of terror, and on submerging the individual in the mass. People in Britain watched these regimes closely, either because they feared them or because they saw them as models to be copied. In the 1930s, almost every democratic system in Europe fell under a dictator or authoritarian ruler. Of these dictators, four stood out:

Adolf Hitler

Hitler was appointed Chancellor of Germany in 1933 and established his position as Führer at the head of the Nazi dictatorship in 1934. By his dynamic policies, a great road building programme and rearmament, Hitler claimed to have eliminated unemployment in Germany by 1938. Many in Britain disapproved of his regime and were afraid of his aggressive foreign policy. Others saw Hitler as a success story and a powerful defence against the spread of Communism.

Benito Mussolini

Mussolini established the first Fascist State in Italy in 1922. Many in Britain admired his supposed social and economic successes and Mussolini had a good image until he invaded Abyssinia in 1935 and entered the Second World War as Hitler's ally in 1940. Mussolini was overthrown in 1943 and finally executed by the Italian resistance in 1945.

Joseph Stalin

Stalin seized control of the Bolshevik State and ruled Soviet Russia from 1928 until 1953. He was responsible for the deaths of millions of his own people, through purges and man-made famine, but few people outside the USSR knew the truth of this at the time. In the 1930s, many British socialists saw Stalin's Russia as a modern, idealistic and progressive society. Many others saw the USSR as a dangerous State determined to promote revolution everywhere, including Britain.

Francisco Franco

Franco led a military revolt against the democratic Spanish republic in 1936 and plunged Spain into three years of vicious civil war. He received some military help from Mussolini and Hitler. The only help the Spanish republicans received was from Stalin's Russia. British opinion was badly divided about Franco's Spain. Many Labour supporters were bitter about Britain not doing more to defend democracy; many others became even more suspicious of Stalin than they were already.

Fig. 5 *European dictators of the 1930s*

The emergence of political extremism in the later 1930s

Severe economic crisis can lead to political extremism and the 1930s did see the triumph of political extremism and of dictatorship in several European countries, notably Germany. Other countries witnessed violent conflict between the political extremes of **communist** and **fascist** parties yet in Britain, though extreme political parties developed, they never got close to power nor did they seriously disrupt national life.

The Communist Party of Great Britain

Founded in 1920, the Communist Party of Great Britain, or CPGB, lasted until the 1990s. Although always small numerically, it had influence beyond its numbers. Members were attracted to it in the 1930s for various reasons. It was based on a distinct philosophy that claimed to provide the working classes and their middle-class supporters with the model for a more equal and progressive society. After a communist regime was established in Russia from 1917, it appeared they were building what British sympathisers called 'a new civilisation'.

Fig. 6 *The NUWM (see page 88) was founded on 15 April 1921 with the appointment of Walter Hannington as national organiser. It was the largest and most confrontational of the groups which emerged to defend the rights of the unemployed during the inter-war period*

(see page 88)

Key terms

Communists: extreme socialists, committed to revolution and class war. From 1917, the Soviet Union was both the first Communist State and the chief backer of communist revolution in Europe.

Fascist: fascist movements developed in several countries, beginning with Mussolini's rise to power in Italy in 1922. Fascism was an ideology based on a strong State, the cult of the leader and subordination of the individual to the national good. It was opposed to democracy, to liberalism and to pacifism. Above all, fascists hated Communism.

Exploring the detail

The Spanish Civil War

Between 1936 and 1939, Spain was convulsed by a vicious civil war. Although its causes lay deep in Spanish history, the war came to be seen as part of a much wider struggle between the forces of Fascism and anti-Fascism. This view was strengthened when Hitler and Mussolini sent aid to the Spanish Nationalist leader, General Franco, and the Soviet Union aided the Spanish Republicans. The Communist Party in Britain not only raised money for the Republican side but encouraged volunteers to join the International Brigade and fight for the Republican cause.

[handwritten: 1 MP IN SCOT & 1 IN WHALES]

[handwritten: NAT. GOV. ↑ BINDS ALL PARTIES CON. LIB. LAB.]

As Capitalism seemed to be collapsing in the early 1930s and parliamentary democracy seemed unable to cope, these revolutionary ideas and the challenge of creating a better type of society from their ruins appealed to many idealistic young people. Faced with mass unemployment, the break up of the Labour government in 1931 and the creation of a British fascist party in 1932, membership of the CPGB rose. The rise of Fascism in Europe also made Communism attractive because it was the communists who seemed to be carrying the fight against Fascism. This was particularly so in the late-1930s with the outbreak of the Spanish Civil War.

How great a threat was the CPGB?

[handwritten: LAB. ABHOR]

Cross-reference

The **Zinoviev Letter** is outlined on page 56.

The Conservative Party often exaggerated the threat from Communism as a way of weakening support for Labour. The classic example of this was the fuss made about the forged Zinoviev Letter in 1924 and the allegations of communist influence behind the General Strike in 1926. Certainly communists were prominent in many aspects of British life in the 1930s. Several trade unions had leaders who were Communist Party members or sympathetic to it. Communists played a key role in major strikes such as in the Lancashire cotton industry in 1932 or the Birmingham rent strike in 1939. Communists also played a leading role in organisations like the National Unemployed Workers' Movement (NUWM) which had 50,000 members in the early 1930s. The NUWM not only gave useful advice to the unemployed but organised 'hunger marches' and mass demonstrations. Some of the latter resulted in violent confrontations with the police.

Cross-reference

The **1934 Incitement to Disaffection Act** is discussed on page 90 [National government policies limiting political extremism].

The CPGB was also active disrupting meetings and marches held by the British Union of Fascists and resulting in violence. The Communist Party newspaper, *The Daily Worker*, had a daily circulation of 80,000 copies, whilst the Left Book Club, in which communist authors were prominent (and was secretly financed by Stalin's USSR), had 50,000 members by 1939. Communists formed a large proportion of the British section of the International Brigade which went to fight in Spain. The CPGB did get a handful of MPs elected – a few Labour MPs were also sympathetic to communist ideas. Party membership doubled in the early 1930s.

Communism also made some headway in the universities, though in most cases these communist loyalties faded away as the students established their careers. One group at Cambridge, called the 'Apostles' however, developed into a network of spies who became notorious when it was revealed in 1951 that they had been passing secrets to the USSR during the war and the early Cold War years. However, although the CPGB certainly had influence, it never posed a really serious threat. Party membership peaked at 18,000. There were never more than one or two communist MPs at any one time. Communist influence in the trade union movement was limited by the opposition of moderate union leaders such as Ernest Bevin. The Labour Party consistently refused to work with the CPGB or allow it to affiliate to the Labour movement. The

Fig. 7 *Oswald Ernald Mosley (1896–1980) successively a Conservative, Independent and Labour MP. Best remembered as leader of the English fascist movement or Black Shirts. Shown here addressing a crowd from the plinth of one of the lions in Trafalgar Square, London. Cartoon from 'Punch', London, 2 November 1932*

[within image: "WITHIN TEN YEARS EUROPE WILL BE EITHER FASCISTS OR FASCITIZED." MUSSOLINI AT MILAN]

[handwritten vertically: STUDENT CENTRAD.]

British Communist Party never had more than a fraction of the strength of its Italian, German or French counterparts.

The National government therefore never felt seriously worried about the CPGB. The secret service kept a close eye on its leaders, sympathisers and activities. The police were not discouraged from cracking down hard on communist led or inspired demonstrations. Legislation such as the 1934 Incitement to Disaffection Act could be used to prosecute communists.

The British Union of Fascists

In October 1932, following a visit to Fascist Italy, Sir Oswald Mosley formed the British Union of Fascists (BUF). Dressed in black uniforms, with a silver flash insignia and giving the fascist salute to the leader, the BUF brought a touch of Italian Fascism to Britain. In 1936, increasing German influence led the movement to be renamed the British Union of Fascists and National Socialists. The BUF gained support from Lord Rothermere, proprietor of the *Daily Mail*, and grew quickly, up to 50,000 members by 1934.

Support for the BUF was strongest in parts of London and in some northern cities like Liverpool, Manchester and Leeds. Early on there was also some support in more affluent middle-class towns like Harrogate – but the typical recruits to the BUF were young working-class men. Supporters varied in their reasons. Mosley was a powerful speaker with ideas for reducing mass unemployment at a time when unemployment was high. His book *The Greater Britain* set out his programme and was thought by some people to be intellectually superior to the writings of Hitler and Mussolini. Mosley played on his ability as an orator. He gave a hundred speeches around the country, published three books and wrote many articles for newspapers and magazines. He was the BUF's biggest asset but also tended to do too much on his own. There were few other talented people in the party.

Between 1931 and 1934, the time looked right for a new political movement. There was inevitable disillusionment with the traditional political parties and system. The collapse of the second Labour government, the failure of the National governments to solve mass unemployment, cuts in government spending and the means test, contrasted with the apparent dynamism of Fascist Italy and Nazi Germany. Mosley's appeal to anti-Semitism won some support in London's East End and in Manchester (anti-Semitism was more politically respectable at that time, before it was discredited by the horrors of the Holocaust) but it was a two-edged sword. For every supporter Mosley gained by exploiting racist attitudes, at least one potential supporter was turned off.

The BUF won some support in the north by arguing for tariffs to protect the declining textile industry. Some traditional Labour supporters flirted with the BUF because they had become disillusioned with Labour in 1931. There was also some support for the BUF from people who were in favour of better relations with Hitler's Germany because they wanted to avoid a war, or thought Hitler was a valuable defence against the evils of Communism.

In the end, Mosley and the BUF never seriously challenged political stability in Britain – but for a brief spell it seemed as if he might do so. Mosley was a credible political figure in the early-1930s. Had the National government broken up in 1933 or 1934, as Labour had done in 1931, then Mosley might have achieved a hold on power. After all, both Mussolini and Hitler had come to power by exploiting times of economic

Exploring the detail

Sir Oswald Mosley – Britain's fascist leader

Mosley entered politics as a Conservative MP in 1918 and was a talented politician. It has been claimed that he could have been party leader of either the Conservatives or of Labour, for whom he was a junior minister in the 1929–31 government.

A brilliant speaker, Mosley gained a strong personal following for his energy and charisma. He put forward innovative ideas to stimulate economic recovery but left Labour in 1931, and established the BUF in 1932 when he seemed to offer leadership and radical policies to solve the crisis of the Depression. After the BUF lost support following violence at its Olympia rally in 1934, Mosley remained prominent in British politics but never again threatened to overturn the established political system.

Cross-reference

More information on **Mosley**, and details of his proposed **economic policies**, can be found on page 68.

Cross-reference

The collapse of the **second Labour government** and the problems of mass **unemployment**, government spending cuts and the **means test** are covered on pages 70–71.

Cross-reference

To recap on **MacDonald** and **Baldwin**, see pages 53 and 54.

Fig. 8 *Sir Oswald Mosley addressing a British Union of Fascists meeting, Manchester, 1933. Note some similarities with European-style Fascism*

and political crisis. Mosley hoped that the same would happen in Britain and that he would be seen as the country's saviour and a formidable rival to the discredited MacDonald and the cautious Baldwin.

Yet his movement never really took off. Even at its peak in 1934, the BUF had a membership of 50,000 – enough to make an impact but far short of a mass movement. By 1935, these numbers declined to 5,000. In the late-1930s there was a modest revival with membership around 20,000 but no political breakthrough came. Electorally, the BUF was a failure with no MPs or even local councillors elected. Following the violence of a BUF indoor rally in London's Olympia Hall in 1934, the BUF lost the support of Lord Rothermere. In the later 1930s, the BUF lost support through becoming more closely associated with the ideals and racial policies of Nazi Germany. Right until the outbreak of war in 1939, Mosley could still attract sizeable audiences to his speeches. The majority attending were opponents determined to disrupt his meetings rather than committed supporters.

National government policies limiting political extremism

National government policies played an important part directly and indirectly in limiting the threat from political extremism. Legislation was passed to curb the activities of both communists and fascists. The 1934 Incitement to Disaffection Act could be used to prosecute anyone advocating revolution or violence of any kind. The Public Order Act 1936 forbade the wearing of political uniforms and gave the police greater powers to control and even to ban political meetings and demonstrations. There were to be no Nuremberg-style rallies in Britain.

The National government itself, with its huge parliamentary majorities in both the 1931 and 1935 general elections, ensured stability and prevented extremist parties from exploiting any power vacuum. It also meant that the government had no need to depend on any political alliances with the extremists. The National government was in place for nine years, in itself a source of stability. In foreign policy, both Stanley Baldwin and Neville Chamberlain (who succeeded Baldwin as prime minister in 1937) avoided coming into conflict with either communist or fascist countries – their policy of 'Appeasement' and the avoidance of war ensured public support at least until March 1939.

Other factors limiting political extremism

The Labour movement also played its part in preventing extremism. In the 1930s, both the party and the trade unions were led by moderates opposed to any link with the communists. Leading trade unionists like Ernest Bevin spent much of their career fighting communist influence

---

■ **Exploring the detail**

The Nuremberg rallies

These were very large and impressive rallies held by the Nazi Party in the German city of Nuremberg. They were designed to create loyalty to Hitler as party leader, as well as to create the image of a strong, organised, dynamic party able to solve the country's problems. Such rallies became a feature of the European dictatorships of the 1930s.

in the trade unions. The Labour Party rejected all attempts by the Communist Party to bring about a '**Popular Front**' against Fascism – as happened in France in 1936 with destabilising effects. Also, despite its terrible defeat in the 1931 election, Labour hung on to its core vote. Although the Conservatives dominated parliament, Labour remained the main opposition party.

International events also discredited the political extremes. By the late-1930s, the truth about Stalin's brutal collectivisation of Soviet agriculture, his show trials of political opponents and his mass purges was beginning to be known. There was also hostility to Stalin's role in the Spanish Civil War. People were even more alienated from Soviet Communism when Stalin made the amazing decision to make a pact with Hitler in August 1939. This took the CPGB completely by surprise and made British communists look both ridiculous and unpatriotic.

Similarly, Mussolini's invasion of Abyssinia in 1935 and his backing for Franco from 1936 turned people away from Fascist Italy. Hitler's Germany was discredited by internal violence, such as **Kristallnacht** 1938, and by his aggression in foreign policy. The outbreak of the Second World War further discredited the BUF. In May 1940, fear that the BUF posed a threat to British security justified Churchill's government in arresting Oswald Mosley and over 700 followers.

Perhaps the most significant factor of all in maintaining stability was the patchy but undeniable economic recovery from 1933–4. One of the popular causes played up by extremists was mass unemployment, for example – but this had been much reduced by 1937. In the Midlands and south east new industries were growing rapidly and a more comfortable lifestyle was developing. Unlike Germany, the British middle classes did not suffer economic disaster. There were pockets of deep unemployment in the depressed areas but these did not lead to political extremism. If anything, the long-term unemployed became demoralised and apathetic, or they adjusted to life on the dole. As George Orwell noted: 'It is quite likely that fish-and-chips, tinned salmon, cut-price chocolate, the movies, the radio, strong tea and the Football Pools have between them averted revolution' (adapted from Orwell, G. (1937) *The Road to Wigan Pier*, Victor Gollancz).

Both the CPGB and the BUF also contributed to their own failure. The communists never found an outstanding leader; there was no British version of Lenin. The BUF had Mosley, but despite his charisma he was impatient, a poor administrator and made political mistakes. Although not all the violence at BUF meetings and marches was due to its members, the BUF got a reputation for thuggery which lost it public support. Finally, there was the continued strength of Britain's political institutions, especially parliament and the monarchy. Unlike Germany and Russia, the 1914–8 war had not ended in defeat and revolution in Britain. There was no widespread loss of faith in parliamentary government nor in constitutional monarchy – not even after the Abdication Crisis of 1936.

Conclusion

Britain in the late-1930s was not free from social and economic problems but was a stable society, relatively confident about the future. The economic crisis of the early-1930s had been blunted if not completely overcome. Political extremism was making a negligible impact within Britain, even if the international situation

■ Activity

Revision exercise

Construct a spider diagram summarising the reasons why extremist movements in Britain posed so limited a threat in the 1930s.

In the central box, summarise key evidence of a communist and fascist threat; then construct a series of boxes around this centre with each summarising one key reason, e.g. role of the National government; international events; economic factors; own weaknesses and mistakes; etc. There should be around six or seven surrounding boxes in total.

was threatening. Foreign observers (including Adolf Hitler) still saw Britain as a great power, with its empire intact. The great smoother-over of difficult situations, Stanley Baldwin, resigned in 1937 but his successor, Neville Chamberlain, was a capable administrator and an impressive politician. Many people (including Chamberlain himself) thought he would make a great prime minister.

In the event, Chamberlain was brought down by his most cherished policy, Appeasement. In May 1940, Chamberlain would have to resign in disgrace. There was no hint of this in 1937 and 1938. Appeasement was seen as the logical policy, supported by the bulk of political and public opinion. When Chamberlain made his flying visits to Germany to negotiate with Hitler and then signed the Munich Agreement, he gained mass popularity. Only a few voices spoke out against Chamberlain at that time – just as only a few voices gave warnings about Britain's social divisions; and only a few voices warned that the British Empire was headed for trouble as colonial independence movements developed.

On the eve of war in 1939, then, it did not seem likely that momentous political, economic or social change was about to take place in Britain. The Second World War made sure that it did.

Fig. 9 *Prime minister Neville Chamberlain (1869–1940) with Hitler and Ribbentrop at Munich, 1938. The contrast in the clothes worn by Chamberlain and Hitler suggests a different attitude to the prospect of another European war*

Learning outcomes

Through your study of this section you should now be familiar with the ways in which underlying problems in the British economy intensified by an unprecedented world Depression affecting British governments and their economic and political policies. You should be able to explain both the economic and political crises of the early 1930s and the consequences of these crises and of government actions.

You should also understand why there was some growth in political extremism in Britain the 1930s and why extremism failed to become a serious threat, as occurred in so many other European countries.

 Examination-style questions

(a) Explain why unemployment was so high in Britain between 1929 and 1935. *(12 marks)*

 For part (a), you are required to write an answer that consists of a series of reasons which are linked and prioritised. As well as the impact of the Wall Street Crash and the financial turmoil of 1931, you will need to link 1930s unemployment to the structural problems of the British economy before 1929. Don't forget to comment on the government's responsibility for unemployment also.

(b) How successful were the governments of the 1930s in bringing about economic recovery in Britain by 1939? *(24 marks)*

 For part (b), you need to evaluate the role of government in helping Britain recover from economic crisis in the 1930s. You will need to consider three themes. First, evidence that government policies did help recovery; second, ways in which government was of only limited or indirect assistance; third, the role of 'other factors'. To reach a judgement, you may wish to think in terms of different areas and times.

7 Britain at war

In this chapter you will learn about:

■ how Churchill emerged as leader of a new coalition government in May 1940

■ the policies and personalities of the coalition government during the war.

Fig. 1 *Reality or myth? David Low cartoon 'All Behind You Winston', May 1940*

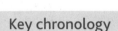

Key chronology

The Second World War, 1939–45

1939 September	German invasion of Poland and outbreak of European War.
1940	Hitler's victories in Scandinavia and the Low Countries. Fall of France.
1941 June	German invasion of the Soviet Union.
1941 December	Japanese attack on Pearl Harbour; US entry into the war.
1944 June	Allied invasion of occupied Europe, via Normandy.
1945 February	Meeting of Churchill, Stalin and Roosevelt at Yalta to plan for the post-war world.
1945 May	VE Day – unconditional surrender of Germany.
1945 August	VJ Day – unconditional surrender of Japan.

Britain's war was in three distinct phases. In the first, from the war's real beginnings with the fall of France in the early summer of 1940 to the start of a real World War with the entry into the war by Japan and the United States in December 1941, Britain stood virtually alone. In the second phase, from the desperate crisis of January 1942 to early-1943 and the 'turn of the tide' in Russia, the Far East, North Africa, and in the Battle of the Atlantic, Britain was a key member of the Grand Alliance with Soviet Russia and the Americans fighting against the 'Axis' of Nazi Germany, Fascist Italy and the empire of Japan. This war remained on a knife edge for most of 1942. By May 1943, however, the ultimate defeat of the Axis could be taken for granted.

In the final phase, from the summer of 1943 to the end of the war in 1945, Germany and Japan were (much more slowly than had been hoped) pounded into defeat by the massive economic and military strength of the rising American and Soviet superpowers. During this phase, Britain became more and more a junior partner in the alliance – and more and more concerned with planning for the post-war world.

Most people in Britain were immensely proud of having 'won' the war, though it would be more precise to say that Britain's great achievement was to keep the war going long enough for the Russians and the Americans to win it. Britain came out of the war with the country badly battered and facing massive debts. Despite this, almost everyone believed the struggle had been worth it. Unlike 1918, the country was not full of a sense of loss and wasted lives. The war had produced a strong sense of unity and purpose. People mostly accepted government restrictions as right and necessary. Most were ready for wartime planning to continue into the work of post-war reconstruction.

Looking back from victory in 1945 to the crisis when Britain was staring at defeat in 1940, two great questions need to be answered. The first is how the British government coped with that crisis and managed the national war effort. The second is how far the impact of the war changed the lives and attitudes of the British people.

The wartime coalition government, May 1940 to May 1945: policies and personalities

From May 1940 until his defeat in the 1945 general election, Winston Churchill led a coalition government that was truly a national one, bringing together politicians from all the leading parties. This coalition proved durable and effective, both in military strategy and in domestic affairs. Many of its key personalities established their political reputations during the war and then went on to have great influence in post-war Britain.

The crises of May 1940 and the formation of the coalition government

Britain was a long way from any thoughts of victory celebrations in May 1940, as the nation faced the threat of invasion and seemed to stand alone in its fight against Nazism. Two interconnected crises were looming. The first one was military – following the disastrous failure of the campaign in Norway and the rapid advances by German forces through France. The second crisis was political – because both the politicians and the people had lost faith in the British prime minister, Neville Chamberlain.

Cross-reference

The **impact of the war** on society and attitudes are discussed on pages 109–19.

Exploring the detail

Military crisis April to May 1940

Britain and France declared war on Germany on 3 September 1939 but there was little fighting in western Europe over the next six months, the time known as the 'phoney war'. Chamberlain hoped that the war would continue to be a limited one, but in April 1940 German troops invaded Denmark and attacked Norway. British troops were sent to Norway but were unable to dislodge the Germans and had to be evacuated. The Norwegian campaign was a humiliating setback. On 10 May 1940, the Germans attacked in western Europe and quickly overran Holland, Belgium and Luxembourg. German forces also made rapid advances against the French. The British Expeditionary Force retreated towards the Channel ports to avoid being encircled. On 25 May, the evacuation of British forces from Dunkirk began.

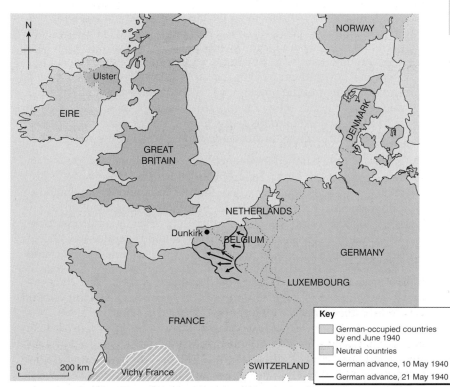

Key

☐ German-occupied countries by end June 1940
☐ Neutral countries
—— German advance, 10 May 1940
—— German advance, 21 May 1940

Fig. 2 *German conquests and occupation in western Europe, April to June 1940*

Key chronology

Britain's war, 1939–40

1939

3 September Chamberlain's declaration of war against Germany.

September 1939 to April 1940 The 'phoney war'.

1940 April Failure of the British military intervention in Norway.

1940 10 May Holland and Belgium overrun by German forces.

Winston Churchill appointed prime minister leading a new government.

1940 May to June German conquest of France.

1940 25 May Commencement of evacuation of British troops from Dunkirk.

1940 22 June Fall of France.

1940 July to September The Battle of Britain.

Autumn 1940 Commencement of the 'Blitz'.

Key terms

Munich Conference: this was held to avert war, following Hitler's demands to take possession of the German-speaking parts of Czechoslovakia. Chamberlain flew to Munich where it was agreed, without Czech consent, that these territories (known as the Sudetenland) should go to Germany. In return, Hitler promised that he had 'no more territorial demands'. Chamberlain believed he had secured 'peace in our time' but Hitler went on to annex all the Czech lands in April 1939 and then attacked Poland in September.

Blockade: using the Royal Navy to 'blockade' Germany by preventing all merchant shipping from entering or leaving German ports had been a major factor in winning the First World War.

Key profile

Neville Chamberlain

Neville Chamberlain, leader of the Conservatives, became prime minister in succession to Stanley Baldwin in 1937. He was seen as a strong and competent leader, with a good record in domestic politics but he will always be remembered for his role in foreign policy, as the architect of the policy known as 'Appeasement' – taking all steps possible to avoid war by using diplomacy to settle Germany's grievances about the 'unfair' peace of 1919. Chamberlain won widespread approval for his determined efforts to avoid another war, especially after the **Munich Conference** in September 1938. Although this apparent success only lasted a few months until Germany tore up the Munich Agreement by occupying Prague and much of Czechoslovakia in March 1939, Chamberlain remained prime minister until May 1940.

When the scale of the military crisis became clear in April 1940, Neville Chamberlain began to face increasing criticism from groups within his own party, from most of the Labour Party, and from the press. There were various reasons for this. His policy of Appeasement had been popular at first but public opinion began to turn against it after Hitler annexed Czechoslovakia in March 1939; and even more so when Germany invaded Poland in September 1939. Chamberlain was also criticised for failing to procure an alliance with Soviet Russia to deter Hitler; and for underestimating Hitler's aggressive intentions. In April 1940, Chamberlain boasted that 'Hitler had missed the bus' – a few days later the Germans invaded Denmark and Norway. This undermined faith in his leadership. Matters came to a head in May 1940.

Chamberlain was heavily criticised for not organising the economy for war with enough urgency. Many MPs felt that the army was inadequately prepared and supplied, and that the **blockade** of Germany was not tight enough. Chamberlain failed to win the support of Labour and form a new National government to fight the war. He even failed to win over all Conservatives. Part of the problem was that Chamberlain did not relish the role of a war leader. 'How I loathe this war. I was never meant to be a War Minister' he wrote to his sister. Defeat and evacuation in Norway, for which he was blamed, further undermined belief in his ability to lead.

On 7 May 1940, Chamberlain opened a debate on the disastrous Norwegian campaign. He faced strong attacks from Conservative backbenchers. The Labour Party demanded that Chamberlain should resign. During this debate, the former prime minister, David Lloyd George, denounced Chamberlain, stating that: 'there is nothing which can contribute more to victory than that he should sacrifice his office.' Conservative rebels refused to support Chamberlain unless Labour and the Liberals were prepared to support the government too. There was no chance of this and Chamberlain duly resigned.

Choosing a new prime minister, May 1940

The two main contenders to replace Chamberlain as prime minister were both Conservatives, Winston Churchill and Lord Halifax. Churchill was a controversial figure. There was hostility towards him from many Conservatives; and, it was widely believed, from the Labour Party. All of the political leaders in 1940 were ready to accept Halifax – Neville Chamberlain and Clement Attlee thought he was actually the better choice of the two. Afterwards, Churchill quickly came to be recognised as the ideal leader – but this was not at all clear at the time. Choosing between the two main candidates was difficult and the result was never a foregone conclusion.

Key profile

Lord Halifax

Lord Halifax had been Viceroy of India in the 1920s and Foreign Secretary in the late-1930s. As Foreign Secretary, he was familiar with the German leadership in Berlin. Many Conservatives, Liberals and even Labour Party members saw him as the best candidate for prime minister in 1940. In the days before the German invasion of Holland and Belgium it was still possible to imagine some form of negotiated deal with Hitler which might prevent the horrors of the 1914–8 war recurring. If Chamberlain resigned, then Halifax was the man most likely to be able to reach an understanding with Hitler.

For others, however, Halifax was far too closely associated with the policy of Appeasement, a policy which had become increasingly discredited during 1939 and whose failure to prevent a European war was now clear. Moreover, as a peer he sat in the House of Lords not in the House of Commons. The last peer to be prime minister had been Lord Salisbury nearly 40 years before. His opponents felt that as a leading appeaser and as a peer he was not the right man to lead a democracy in a great war.

There were also questions about motivation and self-belief. Whereas Churchill was eager to take on the responsibility, convinced that it was his political destiny, Halifax was not at all sure in his own mind that he was the right man for the job – as was revealed in the memoirs of both men:

The morning of the 10th May, 1940, dawned and with it the news that Holland and Belgium had fallen to the Nazi invasion. At eleven o'clock I was again summoned to Downing Street by Mr Chamberlain, the Prime Minister. There I found Lord Halifax the Foreign Secretary. We took our seats and Mr Chamberlain told us that it was beyond his powers to form a National War Coalition government. He had received a reply from the Labour leaders that they would not serve under him. The question, therefore, was whom he should advise the king to send for and ask to form the war Coalition.

There was a long silence. At last Lord Halifax spoke. He felt that his position as a peer, in the Lords and not in the House of Commons, would make it very difficult for him to discharge the duties of a prime minister and especially in wartime. He would be held responsible for everything but would not be able to answer to and guide the Commons. By the time he had finished it was clear that the duty would fall on me.

1   *Adapted from Churchill, W. S.,* **The Gathering Storm***, 1948*

PM said I was the man mentioned as the most acceptable. I said it would be a hopeless position. If I was not in charge of the war and if I didn't lead in the House [of Commons] I should be a cypher. I thought Winston was a better choice. Winston did not demur [disagree]. [He] was very kind and polite but he showed he thought this the right solution.

2   *Adapted from the* **Diary of Lord Halifax** *quoted in Gilbert, M.,* **Winston S. Churchill, Finest Hour***, 1983*

Activity

Thinking point

Using the information in this chapter, pick out the main reasons as to why Chamberlain could not retain the support of the House of Commons in 1940. Explain these reasons.

Cross-reference

Chamberlain's policy of Appeasement is on page 92.

Fig. 3 *Edward Wood, Lord Halifax, (1881–1959)*

Cross-reference

Britain's return to the Gold Standard in 1925 is discussed on page 58.

■ **Key profile**

Winston Churchill

Churchill was famous as a Liberal before the First World War, but had moved to the Conservative Party in 1924. He had then been out of office for over 10 years between 1929 and September 1939 after quarelling with Baldwin and Chamberlain over independence for India, which he was against, and Appeasement. He described the 1930s as his 'wilderness years'. Many in the Labour Party and the trade unions disliked him for his opposition to the General Strike and he had also been associated with a series of past disasters such as the Dardanelles Campaign (also known as Gallipoli) in 1915 and the return to the Gold Standard in 1925. Before 1938–9, Churchill had seemed out of touch with public opinion as well as with his party and most thought that his political career was over. However, he himself had military experience in India, the Sudan and on the Western Front and had been in charge of the Admiralty between 1912 and 1915, helping prepare the Royal Navy for the Great War.

In September 1939, Chamberlain had appointed Churchill to the Admiralty again and during the 'phoney war' only the navy had won any significant victories. In the 1930s, he had also warned of the need for Britain to rearm to meet the German threat especially in the air. Such speeches endeared him to the press and improved his relations with the trade unions and the Labour Party who welcomed his uncompromising opposition to Hitler and Nazism and also his recommendations that trade unions leaders such as Ernest Bevin should be brought into government. Churchill's extensive contacts in the United States were regarded as valuable in order to win US support against Germany and his contributions in parliament, articles in newspapers, historical works and broadcasts on the radio helped give the impression that, despite his age, he was a man of energy and determination.

■ **Activity**

Talking point

1. With reference to the evidence above, explain why Chamberlain chose Churchill to succeed him as prime minister in May 1940.

2. Do you think Chamberlain's choice was a good one? Try to list points that both agree and disagree with this view.

Fig. 4 *Wartime prime minister, Winston Churchill (1874–1965), with characteristic cigar demonstrates his 'common touch'. Unlike Hitler, Churchill made regular visits around the country raising morale and adding to his own legend as an inspirational leader*

Churchill as wartime leader

Churchill faced a terrifying situation in the first weeks of his premiership. By the end of May 1940, German armies were deep into northern France. The British Expeditionary Force was trapped on the Channel coast near Dunkirk and hurried plans had to be made for more than 300,000 men to be evacuated by sea. The fall of France was only a matter of time. This would bring the forces of Nazi Germany within 20 miles of the British coast. An invasion seemed imminent and Britain was alone, apart from the support of the distant empire. There is an excellent account of the crisis facing Churchill at the time of Dunkirk in a short book by John Lukacs, *Five Days In May: London 1940*.

> I would say to the House, as I said to those who have joined this government: 'I have nothing to offer but blood, toil, tears and sweat.'
>
> We have before us an ordeal of the most grievous kind. We have before us many, many long months of struggle and of suffering. You ask, what is our policy? I can say: It is to wage war, by sea, land and air, with all our might and with all the strength that God can give us; to wage war against a monstrous tyranny, never surpassed in the dark, lamentable catalogue of human crime. That is our policy.

3 *Extract from Churchill's first speech as prime minister, 13 May 1940. Quoted in Jenkins, R., **Churchill**, 2001*

What General Weygand called the Battle of France is over.

I expect that the Battle of Britain is about to begin. Upon this battle depends the survival of Christian civilization. Upon it depends our own British life, and the long continuity of our institutions and our Empire. The whole fury and might of the enemy must very soon be turned on us.

Hitler knows that he will have to break us in this Island or lose the war. If we can stand up to him, all Europe may be free and the life of the world may move forward into broad, sunlit uplands.

But if we fail, then the whole world, including the United States, including all that we have known and cared for, will sink into the abyss of a new Dark Age made more sinister, and perhaps more protracted, by the lights of perverted science.

Let us therefore brace ourselves to our duties, and so bear ourselves that, if the British Empire and its Commonwealth last for a thousand years, men will still say, 'this was their Finest Hour'.

4   *Extract from Churchill's speech, 18 June 1940. Quoted in Jenkins, R., **Churchill**, 2001*

However, not everyone saw things in Churchill's way. Lord Halifax and other Conservatives felt that, with France collapsing, an army retreating to Dunkirk, no help from America and Germany controlling most of western Europe, the sensible policy was to negotiate with Hitler. They regarded Churchill's speeches as emotional bravado and believed that Britain would be better getting what terms it could rather than being invaded and conquered. So they favoured a compromise peace. It was a measure of Churchill's self-confidence that he convinced most of his cabinet and the population that it was better to fight on in the hope that the United States could be persuaded to support Britain. He said to his cabinet:

I have thought carefully in these last days whether it was part of my duty to consider entering into negotiations with That Man [Hitler]. But it was idle to think that if we tried to make peace now, we should get better terms than if we fought it out. The Germans would demand our Fleet – that would be called 'disarmament' – our naval bases and much else. We should become a slave state, though a British Government which would be Hitler's puppet would be set up – 'under Mosley or some such person'. And where should we be at the end of all that?

5   *Quoted in Charmley, J., **Churchill: the End of Glory**, 1993*

Rather than seek peace, Churchill put everything into organising the military effort against Nazi Germany. In the summer of 1940, as the Germans made invasion preparations to cross the Channel, everything depended upon control of the skies. The aerial battles of the 'Battle of Britain' in the summer of 1940 between the Luftwaffe and a few hundred Royal Air Force pilots were the key to Britain's survival. By late September, it was evident that the Luftwaffe had failed to gain complete control in the air; Hitler's attention switched

Activity

Talking point

Churchill's speeches had a tremendous impact on MPs in the House of Commons at the time and, later, on the public when they were published.

1 Read Sources 3 and 4 taken from two of Churchill's most famous speeches in 1940 (or better still listen to a recording) and consider why they had such an impact. Analyse the ways Churchill used language, the emotions his speeches appealed to, and the themes you can detect.

2 Decide how far you agree with the comment by the American journalist, Ed Murrow, that Churchill 'mobilised the English language and sent it into battle'. Note, however, that not all of his speeches were broadcast by Churchill in person. Some of them were read out by a BBC announcer.

Cross-reference

Further information on **Sir Oswald Mosley** is given on pages 89–90.

towards plans for the invasion of Soviet Russia. This was what Churchill called the 'Finest Hour' – the time when Britain stood alone and ensured that the war would last long enough for others to join in.

During and after the war, Winston Churchill became a legend. His inspiring leadership was credited with unifying the nation. But Churchill also had his faults. He was impulsive, dictatorial, constantly interfered in the details of government departments, thought he knew more about strategy and tactics than his generals and was a poor committee chairman. Even those devoted to him noted these and other failings. His cabinet under-secretary remembered him as 'not at all kind and considerate. He was exacting beyond reason and could be ruthlessly critical'. Sir Robert Menzies, the Australian prime minister, who admired Churchill hugely, noted during the war that 'he is not interested in finance, economics or agriculture and ignores the debates on all three. He loves war, and spends hours with maps and charts' (diary of R. Menzies, 26 April 1941). The Chief of the General Staff, General Brooke, was very critical of Churchill, often to his face, for making impetuous and unrealistic decisions.

Churchill was lucky in his deputy prime minister, Clement Attlee, a man with little or no charisma but an extremely effective organiser. A letter from Attlee to Churchill during the war shows up the differences between the two men: 'When reports do come before Cabinet, it is very exceptional for you to have read them', Attlee wrote. 'Often, you have not even read the notes which have been prepared for your guidance. The result is long delays and unnecessarily long Cabinet meetings' (adapted from Jenkins, R. (2002) *Churchill*, Pan Books). Such negative impressions as these led several of Churchill's biographers, such as Clive Ponting, to put forward a very critical, 'revisionist' view of his record as war leader. In recent years, however, there has been a swing back in Churchill's favour, especially in the 2005 BBC television series *Great Britons* and in two admiring biographies, *Churchill* by Roy Jenkins, and *Churchill: A Study in Greatness* by Geoffrey Best.

Churchill's wartime coalition government

On becoming prime minister, Churchill's first task was to form a new government. Given the desperate situation unfolding across the Channel this needed to be a government of national unity. Although Churchill was prime minister, Chamberlain continued to be the leader of the Conservative Party until his death in November 1940. This made it easier for Churchill to act as if he were above party politics and to bring into government Labour and Liberal politicians as well as Conservatives. Churchill also brought in talented individuals from outside the political parties. His 1940 war cabinet consisted of Churchill himself, Clement Attlee (Labour), Arthur Greenwood (Labour), Neville Chamberlain (Conservative) and Lord Halifax (Conservative). During the course of the war, other key figures included Ernest Bevin, Anthony Eden, Lord Beaverbrook, Sir Kingsley Wood, Sir John Anderson and Lord Woolton.

In addition to those shown in the photograph, others made important contributions to Churchill's government – as well as Conservatives, two Liberal ministers were appointed and 14 Labour politicians at various levels of government. Churchill also brought in men with experience outside Westminster. Three important examples of this wide range of talents were Herbert Morrison, Lord Woolton, and William Beveridge.

AQA Examiner's tip

Churchill referred to his war coalition government as a National government and so Conservative posters in 1945 often read 'Vote National'. Do not confuse this National government with the one in the 1930s.

Arthur Greenwood

Greenwood became deputy-leader of the Labour Party in the 1930s and was an outspoken critic of Appeasement. As Attlee's deputy, he was invited to join Churchill's war cabinet in May 1940. He was dropped from the war cabinet in 1943 and put in charge of plans for reconstruction.

Ernest Bevin

Ernest Bevin founded and led the largest trade union, the Transport and General Workers; he played a key role in the Labour movement between the wars. Bevin's opposition to both Communism and Fascism, together with his organisational skills, won Churchill's admiration. He was Minister of Labour and for National Service from 1940 to 1945 and proved crucial to maximising economic output. After 1945 he was foreign secretary under Attlee.

Lord Beaverbrook

Max Aitken, Lord Beaverbrook, was a Canadian who turned the *Daily Express* into one of the most influential newspapers in Britain. Beaverbrook was an individualist, not fitting easily into any party or government. Churchill recruited Beaverbrook into the government, where his greatest contribution to the war effort was as Minister of Aircraft Production, greatly expanding the number of aeroplanes available to the RAF.

Kingsley Wood

Kingsley Wood was Minister for Air 1938–40 and Chancellor of the Exchequer 1940–3. To pay for the war, Kingsley Wood raised taxation though some of this was to be credited to taxpayers and returned after the war. Wood later developed the 'Pay-As-You-Earn' system for income tax.

Sir John Anderson

John Anderson became Home Secretary in 1940 (the Anderson air-raid shelter for use in gardens was named after him). In 1943, he succeeded Kingsley Wood as Chancellor of the Exchequer.

Winston Churchill

Winston Churchill became prime minister in May 1940 remaining in office until the general election in the summer of 1945. Not only did he preside over the war cabinet but he acted as his own Minister of Defence, exercising considerable control over war strategy, as well as devising his own foreign policy. Churchill periodically intervened in other policy areas such as propaganda but had much less interest in social reform. One government department where he did not intervene was the Ministry of Labour. This, Churchill left to Ernest Bevin.

Clement Attlee

Clement Attlee acted as deputy prime minister to Churchill and much of the administration of domestic matters was conducted by him. He presided over cabinet meetings and was a highly effective chairman. This raised his stature amongst his political colleagues in and out of the Labour Party. Attlee also helped to persuade Churchill to accept various principles of social reform. He became prime minister in 1945.

Anthony Eden

Eden was foreign secretary from 1935 until he resigned in protest against Appeasement in 1938. He was again foreign secretary from 1940 to 1945. Churchill had great admiration for Eden and recommended him to King George VI as his successor, should he himself be killed. Eden became prime minister in 1955.

Fig. 5 *'Churchill's war cabinet, latter part of 1940. Left to right standing: Arthur Greenwood, Minister without Portfolio; Ernest Bevin, Minister of Labour and National Service; Lord Beaverbrook, Minister of Aircraft Production; Sir Kingsley Wood, Chancellor of the Exchequer. Left to right sitting: Sir John Anderson, Lord President of the Council; Winston Churchill, First Lord of the Treasury and Minister of Defence; Clement Attlee, Lord Privy Seal; Anthony Eden, Secretary of State for Foreign Affairs*

Key profiles

Herbert Morrison

Herbert Morrison became Labour leader of the London County Council in 1934. He was responsible for creating an integrated public transport system for London and with the policy of the 'green belt' to save the countryside from the endless spread of London's suburbs. In 1940, he was appointed Minister of Supply and took over as Home Secretary in 1943. He was responsible for security on the Home Front, including voluntary organisations for civil defence, such as Air Raid Precautions and the National Fire Service.

Lord Woolton

The Earl of Woolton was a successful businessman from Manchester who became Minister of Food in 1940 under Churchill. Woolton gained respect for his management of the system of rationing. After the war, he played a key role in modernising the Conservative Party's organisation and in winning the 1951 election.

William Beveridge

William Beveridge was an expert on unemployment and social insurance. He had advised Churchill and Lloyd George on their welfare reforms before 1914. Between the wars he was an academic teaching at the London School of Economics and Oxford. In 1941, Arthur Greenwood set up a committee to consider changes in the national insurance scheme. Beveridge then drew up a report in 1942 which went far beyond looking at minor wartime changes but instead proposed a whole new system of welfare based on social insurance.

Cross-reference

The Beveridge Report of 1942 is covered on pages 106–7.

Churchill's wartime coalition proved to be stable and efficient. It did not split the Conservative Party in the way Lloyd George had split the Liberals in 1916. One reason for this was the absence of major rivals to Churchill. Illness drove Chamberlain out of office and Halifax was sent as ambassador to the United States. The Conservatives, as the largest party in parliament, had 52 posts in government compared to Labour's 16. Some Conservative MPs resented the number of posts given to Labour but Churchill realised the importance of having Labour and trade union support both for political reasons and for the war economy.

As the war went on, Labour's strength in the government increased. By 1945, it held 27 posts, mainly to do with the Home Front where it dominated economic and social affairs. This experience of government and being in the public eye were eventually to be key factors in its great victory in the 1945 general election. Labour was seen as having made a big contribution to the success of the war effort. Labour was not blamed for the near disaster at Dunkirk, the closeness of Nazi invasion and the bombing of London and other cities in the Blitz. By contrast, popular opinion was ready to blame the Conservative-dominated governments of the 1930s for having failed in their foreign and defence policies. This, too, was to influence the result of the 1945 general election.

Policies of the wartime coalition government

The wartime coalition government had three main tasks:

1 Organising the economy for war.
2 Paying for the war.
3 Planning for post-war Britain.

Organising the war economy

As soon as war broke out, the Emergency Powers (Defence) Act 1939 was passed, by which the government was granted authority to make regulations covering any aspect of life necessary to secure the defence of the realm. Hundreds of regulations were issued under this act during the war. Government became much more centralised. Ministries were set up for food and shipping, information and economic warfare. A Ministry of Aircraft Production and a Ministry of Labour were established, followed in 1942 by a Ministry of Production. Cabinet committees coordinated the work of the separate ministries with the Ministry of Production coordinating on the supply side and the Treasury being responsible for finance. One key issue was the control of the supply of labour for key industries. Ernest Bevin, the Minister of Labour, oversaw the allocation of labour. Bevin had a long career in trade union affairs before the war. In many ways, he was the ideal choice as Minister of Labour. There were still over a million unemployed in 1940 and Bevin not only had to get them back to work but mobilise the workforce efficiently for total war.

A closer look

Ernest Bevin and the organisation of war work

Ernest Bevin was given enormous powers over Britain's workforce. After the war, his counterpart in Nazi Germany, Albert Speer, said that Bevin had far greater control over the supply of labour in democratic Britain than Speer had ever had in Nazi Germany. Bevin enjoyed his power over labour and used it well. He had to oversee the allocation of man and woman power among the competing demands of armed forces, industry, agriculture, war work, civil defence and normal civilian services. Military conscription had already been introduced, but Bevin added industrial conscription for men and later for women too.

Bevin's ministry could direct anyone to work at any job in any place. From late-1943, for example, young men, the so-called 'Bevin Boys', were conscripted for work in the coal mines, while women were encouraged to work in munitions, engineering and shipbuilding industries. The demands of war production soon mopped up unemployment. Even though 4.5 million entered the armed forces, the total workforce rose by 2 million.

Bevin used 'essential work orders' to force factories to improve conditions, for example through works canteens, washrooms and medical centres. Wages were improved, and trade union bargaining continued despite restrictions on strikes. Bevin also paid close attention to maintaining workers' morale. He constantly toured factories, delivering over 300 speeches to workers and managers, and encouraged lunchtime entertainment in the factories which from 1941 was broadcast on BBC radio as 'Workers' Playtime'.

Bevin's contribution to the war effort did a lot to change public perceptions and to convince people that Labour politicians could be trusted with power.

Due in part to Bevin's work, Britain showed how a free society could mobilise its workforce for war. However, there were limits to what could be achieved. In the coal industry, still the main source of Britain's fuel and power, total output and productivity remained disappointing. Many miners were attracted into other wartime jobs or joined the forces. Too many coal mines were old, lacked modern machinery and were both dangerous and inefficient. As a result, Britain had to rely heavily on imports of oil, making the economy vulnerable to the effects of U-boat attacks on shipping.

To maximise war production, priority had to be given to imports of essential raw materials and machinery. Given the loss of shipping due to German U-boat attacks, imports of food had to be reduced. In turn, this meant the rationing of food, clothing, fuel, etc. Basic foods were rationed from 1940 and most others by 1941. Devising a fair rationing policy and advising the public on how to make the best of it was the work of the Ministry of Food under Lord Woolton.

As in the First World War, government control was extended over industry both directly and indirectly. The Royal Ordnance Factories employed 300,000 workers, whilst another 265 factories did work for the Admiralty and the Ministry of Aircraft Production. Non-essential industries were run down so that their machinery and labour could be diverted to war work. New production methods were devised in order to raise output and save labour. The government also encouraged greater use of science, both for improving the efficiency of the economy and for developing new techniques of warfare.

Agriculture was encouraged to increase home food output. Millions of acres of land were ploughed up, production shifted from meat to cereals and greater use was made of fertilisers and tractors to raise productivity. A major 'Dig for Victory' campaign led to a huge rise in home-grown vegetables in back gardens, allotments, and sports fields.

Paying for the war

For Britain, the Second World War lasted six years, half as long again as the 1914–8 war. Paying for it was a major problem. The war cut earnings from exports and from overseas investments which had to be sold off. Although Britain had gold and dollar reserves, these were all spent out by 1941. The economy was heavily dependent on American loans.

The coalition government tried to pay for war by:

■ squeezing consumption through high taxation, rationing and persuading the public to buy **war bonds**

■ neglecting new investment in any area except for war production

■ relying on overseas aid from the empire and the United States.

Income tax went up to 10 shillings (50p) in the pound and nearly all workers now paid income tax. To make collection easier and fairer, the Pay-As-You-Earn system was introduced in 1943. Indirect taxes on goods and services were also raised partly to bring in more money but also to help ration the supply of materials and labour.

■ **Cross-reference**

Ernest Bevin's and Lord Woolton's roles are discussed in connection with the key personalities of the war cabinet on pages 101–2.

Fig. 6 *Second World War poster*

■ **Key term**

War bonds: government borrowing to be paid back after the war. In total, the public lent £8,500 million to the State to help pay for the war.

Canada provided a particularly generous gift of $1,000 million as well as interest free loans. Other empire countries sent materials in return for IOUs to be paid after the war. The United States agreed the Lend-Lease scheme in 1941, by which it provided war materials and essential supplies which would be returned or paid for at a later date. Lend-Lease proved vital in helping Britain pay for the war, providing £27,000 million of aid in total.

In effect, Britain paid for the Second World War like the First, partly by higher taxation but largely through internal and external borrowing. However, it became very dependent upon Lend-Lease and empire aid and its exports were no longer able to pay for more than a fraction of its imports. By 1945, Britain faced massive debts.

Planning for post-war Britain

Although the immediate threat of a German invasion was over by 1941, the war continued to go badly for Britain in 1942. Japan overran many of Britain's possessions in the Far East. In North Africa, German forces reversed earlier British successes against the Italians. In the Atlantic, German U-boats threatened Britain's supply line to North America. The war only turned in Britain's favour between November 1942 and May 1943. Even so, plans to tackle Britain's social problems were begun as early as 1941. Once it was clear ultimate victory was assured, these plans were published and debated. Political and public attitudes towards planning changed.

Several factors helped to cause this change. One was the need to maintain morale during the worst period of the war. In 1940–2, politicians wanted to be able to offer hope that there would soon be a better Britain for everyone. By 1943–4, as victory became certain, the public became increasingly impatient to know what improvements could be expected after the war. Outside pressure also forced the government to respond. For example, in February 1941 the TUC sent a deputation to the Ministry of Health pointing out the defects in the national health insurance system and asking for its reform. A series of articles, radio talks, official reports, and publications by leading churchmen, all created a demand for planning reforms for post-war Britain.

The war itself forced change. Fear of mass bombing led to the Emergency Hospital Scheme, giving the State greater central control over hospitals as well as providing free treatment for bomb victims. Rationing enabled the State to provide free milk and extra food resources to children and mothers. Common danger encouraged a more generous attitude towards social welfare – the hated 'means test' was abolished in 1941. All three political parties set up their own committees to examine key issues of reconstruction. Between 1942 and 1945, a whole series of reports, and acts of parliament were issued by the coalition government. Some changes, such as the 1944 Education Act, were made before the 1945 election but most of the wartime promises for social reform and a 'better Britain' were eventually carried out by Attlee's post-war Labour governments.

There were many proposals for a 'better Britain'. The economist J. M. Keynes put forward new ideas for avoiding inflation and unemployment. A government White Paper in May 1944 entitled 'Employment Policy' committed future governments to ensure 'a high and stable level of employment', as well as post-war controls to prevent the returning troops facing unemployment, as had happened in 1918.

Activity

Talking point

What economic and financial problems was Britain likely to face once the war ended?

Cross-reference

The reforms of the **Attlee government** are detailed on page 131.

Several government measures were taken during the war to implement these promises. The education minister, R. A. Butler, and his civil servants drew up plans for the 1944 Education Act. This provided a form of free, compulsory secondary education. The school leaving age was to be raised to 15 immediately and 16 later. Local authority grants for fees and maintenance would be available to students who qualified for university entrance.

Key profiles

R. A. Butler

Butler was the Conservative President of the Board of Education from 1941–45. Butler drew up and took through parliament the 1944 Education Act, making maintained secondary education free and compulsory. He played a major role in the revival of the Conservative party after its defeat in 1945, and was a senior figure in the party in the 1950s and early 1960s.

Henry Willink

Willink was the Conservative Minister for Health in Churchill's wartime government. He drew up plans for a national health service but was not able to implement them due to the Conservative defeat in the 1945 election.

A White Paper entitled 'A National Health Service' was published in 1944 by Henry Willink, the Minister of Health (Conservative), after much discussion with Labour ministers and the medical profession. There was much disagreement on the details, and implementing the plans after the war proved very controversial. But key principles were set out for the future – that everyone irrespective of their means should have equal access to medical services, that the health service should cover all forms of treatment, and that hospital care would be free at the point of delivery.

A Ministry for Town and Country Planning was set up in 1943. The 1944 Town and Country Planning Act gave local authorities powers to deal with blitzed or slum areas needing redevelopment. In 1945, the Family Allowances Act was passed. This had been promoted by Labour MPs and by Eleanor Rathbone, a feminist reformer and independent MP who had campaigned for help for mothers. It provided a weekly benefit of five shillings (25p) for the second child and subsequent children. It was a universal benefit not subject to any means test. The State had accepted responsibility for making a financial contribution to the cost of bringing up every family of two or more children regardless of the parents' means.

These measures formed part of what would become known as the 'welfare state', associated in the public mind with William Beveridge and his famous Beveridge Report published in December 1942, showing how poverty could be conquered through a system of social insurance backed up by a free health service and full employment.

A closer look

The Beveridge Report, 1942

The White Paper known as the Beveridge Report was published in December 1942, entitled 'Social Security and Allied Services'. Compiled by William Beveridge, it sold over 600,000 copies.

Beveridge wrote of 'slaying the Five Giants' which caused poverty – want, sickness, lack of education, bad housing, and unemployment. The press and public seized on the Report's more revolutionary aspects, such as its proposals for a national health service, family allowances and the maintenance of a high level of employment. The Report itself referred to the need for a revolution in the welfare system, and radical aspects included making national insurance universal and comprehensive; having a single weekly insurance contribution covering health, unemployment and old age pension; having all benefits administered by a single government department – the Ministry of Social Security; the end of means testing and providing a universal national minimum benefit for everyone from birth to death.

In fact, the Beveridge Report was less revolutionary than people believed. Many of Beveridge's ideas were similar to those of the New Liberals before 1914. For example, benefits would be at subsistence level only, individualism was still to be cherished despite the increased role of the State, and Beveridge did not explain how a high employment rate was to be maintained. His view of the family was rooted in the past; for example he assumed that most women would not work outside the home after marriage.

Fig. 7 *The Beveridge Report was published in December 1942, coinciding with a British Commonwealth victory at El Alamein*

Cross-reference

To review **New Liberalism**, see page 16.

It contained, therefore, continuity as well as change, and was only a plan, though it quickly developed momentum. Churchill's fears that it would prove too expensive and raise expectations too high were in some ways justified; but for the generation which had lived through the Depression of the 1930s and the terrors of the Second World War, Beveridge offered a vision of a safe, secure and prosperous future which made the war worth fighting. In 1944, a government White Paper entitled 'Social Insurance' accepted most of Beveridge's proposals and a Ministry of National Insurance was set up.

The successes and failures of the wartime coalition

The wartime coalition government did not succeed in everything. There were many military disasters, such as the humiliating surrender of Singapore in 1942. There were occasionally intense disagreements within the cabinet, and many criticisms of Churchill. There was opposition from independently minded Labour MPs, such as Aneurin Bevan and also from several women MPs from all parties who stood up for women's interests. The biggest revolt was in support of a back bench Labour motion critical of the government's negative reaction to the Beveridge Report. Churchill had to face down more than one vote of no confidence proposed in the House of Commons. Behind the wartime propaganda image of national unity, there was frequent grumbling and sarcastic jokes about government mistakes and inefficiencies.

Despite all this, the Churchill coalition proved remarkably strong. This strength reflected national unity arising out of the extreme danger that

Cross-reference

Aneurin Bevan is profiled on page 137.

Britain faced and from Churchill's personal charisma. However, there were other factors. Labour's leaders were fully absorbed in government work and many of them came to admire Churchill a lot. An electoral truce was agreed between the parties. The government was also energetic and capable and held together until almost the end of the war. There was broad agreement in certain areas but real differences of principle in others. There were deep divisions over plans for nationalisation of land and industry. This prevented agreement on the future of essential industries like coal and the railways, and on public utilities like gas and electricity even though two-thirds of these industries were already owned by local authorities.

There were also differences over how far State controls over the economy should be prolonged after the war. The Conservatives accepted that some would be needed for a while as the post-war economy adjusted to peace, while Labour wanted to retain many controls permanently. The details of a future national health service proved controversial. There were divisions between the main parties over the nationalisation of hospitals, whether doctors should become State employees and whether medical treatment should be free for everyone or only for those too poor to pay. Not only were there divisions between the parties but also within them. When the post-war Labour government went about setting up the new National Health Service, it faced considerable opposition.

Even when there was agreement there were differences over details. The Labour left wing argued that reforms were not going far enough. They were critical of the 1944 Education Act for not abolishing private schools. There were also Labour criticisms of the Beveridge proposals for national insurance. Critics felt that flat-rate contributions were unfair to the lower paid and that benefits were too low. Similarly, family allowances and old age pensions were criticised as inadequate. Many Conservatives, on the other hand, claimed the plans for reform were much too radical and expensive. At the head of the government, Churchill failed to give a clear lead in domestic policies and was not always encouraging to the reformers. His lack of commitment to domestic affairs and his reluctance to promise the British people too much cost him many votes in the 1945 election.

■ **Cross-reference**

The work of the Labour government in setting up the post-war **National Health Service** is covered on pages 136–7.

The **1945 election** is discussed on page 121.

■ **Summary questions**

1. How successful was the wartime coalition government in leading Britain through the strains of war between 1940 and 1945?

2. How far was Churchill personally responsible for maintaining national morale?

8 A social revolution? Total war and social upheaval

In this chapter you will learn about:

- the effect of the wartime government's policies on British society

- the impact of 'total war' on the civilian population on the Home Front

- the extent of social change in Britain by 1945.

Who's next? Says the Sprouting Broccoli. Onions, tomatoes and potatoes have all disappeared from time to time. Health-giving green vegetables may also become scarce, unless you grow them yourselves – women and older children as well as men. Make sure of your family's supply of greens all through the year, from your garden.

DIG FOR VICTORY NOW!

1 *Propaganda poster from the Ministry of Agriculture, 1942*

Carrot Flan reminds you of Apricot Flan, but it has a deliciousness all its own.

2 *Ministry of Food advertisement, 1941*

A woman from Middlesbrough was fined after being found guilty of wasting food. The court heard that she threw buttered slices of bread into the garden. It was the first charge of its kind heard in the town under the Waste of Food Order.

3 *Report in the Middlesbrough Evening Gazette, 3 February 1942*

These three sources, from 1940–2, give brief, random glimpses of life in wartime Britain. They will be easily remembered by anyone who lived through the war. They reveal the intensity of government propaganda and the extent to which the State intervened in the small details of people's lives. For Britain, the Second World War was indeed a 'total war' bringing all civilians into a sense of shared struggle and sacrifices. For huge numbers of people, the war was a life-changing experience, for good or bad.

The Second World War lasted longer than the First World War, involved civilians on a much greater scale and led the State to take far wider powers than ever before. No one escaped the impact of war, although this varied according to social class, age, gender and region. The impact of this war on people's lives was much greater than just the effects of government policies. In all sorts of ways, directly and indirectly, the war changed people's lives.

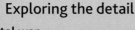

Exploring the detail

Total war

'Total war' is a war which involves everyone and in which the State controls and organises the entire resources of the country including its human resources. Its purpose is to mobilise all resources in an all-out effort to win. During the Second World War the British State took a greater degree of control over its people and their property than in any other country except Soviet Russia. By the Emergency Powers (Defence) Act 1939, parliament gave the government authority to make regulations covering any aspect of life necessary to secure the defence of the realm. Hundreds of regulations were issued under this act during the war.

The impact of total war upon society and attitudes

Breaking down class barriers

The impact of the war was felt right across British society. One aspect was social mobility – the way the war took people out of their local communities and scattered them far and wide across Britain and across

Fig. 1 *Princess Elizabeth being shown vehicle maintenance*

■ **Cross-reference**

To refresh your knowledge of **conscription** during the First World War, see page 39.

■ **Exploring the detail**

The Home Guard

The Home Guard was formed in May 1940 in response to the threat of invasion. By June 1940, 1.5 million had volunteered. It was an unpaid 'people's army' combining men from all classes who were under 18, over 65 or in a reserved occupation. Although later disparaged as 'Dad's Army', it played important roles. The Guard released regular servicemen from having to guard the coastline, factories and aerodromes and assisted with Civil Defence. It had units trained in sabotage and guerrilla warfare and acted as a training ground for boys prior to call-up. The Home Guard was stood down in 1944 and disbanded in 1945.

the world. Military conscription was introduced in September 1940, with all men aged 18 to 41 liable to be called up, although there were exemptions for those in vital war work and for conscientious objectors. Serving in the armed forces took men who had never even dreamed of travelling abroad to the deserts of North Africa, to convoy protection in the Atlantic Ocean, to Malta, Burma, Italy and hundreds of other faraway places. Older men took on new responsibilities as they were conscripted into 'national service' as special constables, firewatchers, or workers in Civil Defence or the Home Guard. Unmarried women between 19 and 30 could also be conscripted, although they were given a choice between service in the Women's Auxiliary Forces or war work in industry. The war turned young women into factory workers, bus drivers, nurses and codebreakers. Before the war, many of these girls would never have thought of leaving home until they got married.

By mid-1941 the army, navy and airforce between them had over 3 million young men in uniform, of whom over a million were volunteers. By 1944, the size of the armed forces had risen to over 4.5 million, plus nearly half a million in the women's services. In addition to the regular armed forces, the Home Guard numbered 1.75 million men by 1943. Alongside the British armed forces, there were large contingents from empire countries like Canada and the West Indies, from European nations under Nazi occupation such as the Free French, Czechs, Poles and Norwegians and, from 1942 onwards, vast numbers of American servicemen. By 1944, there were over 1.5 million overseas troops stationed in Britain.

The war amounted to almost a mass migration of people, civilians as well as soldiers. Young people mixed with, fell in love with and often married other young people they would never have met or heard of in peacetime – Polish pilots, American GIs, German refugees, youngsters evacuated from the inner cities to temporary homes in the country. The social consequences of all this were sometimes beneficial, widening people's social horizons and leading them towards a better life. Other effects were much more painful – petty crime, bereavements, broken marriages, and the ethnic violence among American servicemen in Lancashire and other places in 1943.

The war banished some pre-war evils. Despite shortages and rationing, nutrition standards in many working-class families actually improved. Unemployment, still over a million in 1939, fell by half during 1939–42 and had virtually disappeared by 1943. Full employment was available even in the areas that had been worst off during the 1930s. Women poured into the munitions factories and other forms of war work. On the other hand, not everyone enjoyed being directed into certain jobs. Those who had previously worked in service jobs found factory work noisy and dirty; so too did the 20,000 young men directed into coal mining as 'Bevin Boys'. There was resentment of the 'spivs' who exploited the opportunities offered by the black market and petty crime.

War work often involved 11- or 12-hour working days and also night working. Along with other activities such as firewatching or the Home Guard, this left little time for a social life. Tiredness partly explains the rise in industrial accidents, with a thousand a year proving fatal. The right to strike was subject to severe legal restraint through compulsory arbitration. There were some strikes, notably in coal mining and engineering, but fewer than 2 million working days were lost through strikes between 1940 and 1945 compared with over 5 million during the 1914–8 war. The status of trade unions rose. Membership increased from 6.3 million to 8.9 million.

The combination of full employment, overtime and piece rate work raised average earnings for the working classes. The average male weekly earnings rose by 80 per cent between 1938–45, while average earnings for female workers almost doubled. Together with rationing of essential foods and controls on prices, rents and profits, this increased the relative standard of living of the working class. Not everyone gained. The wives and families of serving men, of which there were over 4 million by 1944, lost out. Servicemen's pay was relatively low and there was no overtime or piece work. The middle and upper classes were hit by high taxation, death duties and limits on profits which could be made from factories or land.

The house-building boom of the 1930s was halted once war broke out. Labour, money and materials were needed for war work. 220,000 houses had been completed in 1939–40, but this dropped to 7,000 by 1943. On top of this, German bombing raids damaged or destroyed around 4 million houses. London's East End suffered the most damage but other towns and cities such as Plymouth and Manchester, and the Midlands, particularly Birmingham and Coventry, were badly hit. Bombing killed over 60,000 British civilians, seriously injured another 86,000, and made over 2 million temporarily homeless. People who had been bombed out were sent to 'rest centres' in schools or church halls but conditions were often poor. Real-life experience rarely matched the cosy images of official propaganda. There was often resentment in working-class areas against middle-class people who could drive out to safety in the country.

■ **Cross-reference**

More information on **Ernest Bevin's** work as Minister of Labour can be found on page 103.

Some women worked as code breakers at **Bletchley Park**. As in earlier wars, thousands of women entered nursing both at home and close to the various Fronts.

'Land Girls' served in the Women's Land Army, filling the gaps caused by agricultural workers being called up to the armed forces. A 1998 film *Land Girls*, based on the novel by Angela Huth, provides a fictional portrayal of their experiences.

It is sometimes said that the war caused a 'sexual revolution'. Certainly there is some evidence for this. Moral constraints were loosened by the circumstances of the war. Many young women found themselves living away from home, in close proximity to a lot of young men in uniform. One woman looking back after the war, said serving in the WRNS 'was like one never-ending shipboard romance'. The war intensified emotions and seemed to make life happen faster. Even 'nice girls' were less likely to 'say no' when they knew they might never see the young man again after that night, because his unit would be moved somewhere else or because his plane might be shot down the next day.

Sexual relationships did not only flourish among the young people who had found themselves far from home. Many housewives found themselves alone and neglected and formed liaisons with other men instead. Broken marriages were common. After the war, most women kept quiet about their wartime sexual experiences – but in the looser social climate of the 1990s, now as grandmothers, they started to reveal the truths hidden behind their very respectable lives. A Channel Four TV documentary *What Granny Did In The War* provides a fascinating collection of no-holds-barred reminiscences.

As with all so-called social revolutions, the problem with the impact of the Second World War on the roles and attitudes of women lies in deciding what was typical, or not, and what was lasting change rather than a temporary interruption to the normal rhythms of social life. It is perfectly possible to argue that the war changed attitudes and paved the way for major advances for women. But it is equally possible to put up a convincing argument that the vast majority of women accepted their traditional role as wives and mothers after 1945 and throughout the 1950s, with the real sexual revolution having to wait until the 1960s.

Myths and realities: propaganda images of Britain at War

As seen through official propaganda films and posters, through the cosy images of newspapers, films and light entertainment at the time, and the rosy memories recounted after the war, wartime Britain was united, patriotic and free of class war. For many people, then and since, Britain experienced a 'good war'. Many of the propaganda myths were true – or at least close to the truth. Others were very different from reality. During the Blitz, people were told, and mostly believed, that they all rallied round in a spirit of comradeship and sharing. But this was not always the case. Newsreel film of the worst casualties and damage was never shown. Survivors of bombing raids often shouted abuse at dignitaries visiting the ruins – naturally such incidents were covered up. There were occasions of panic, also not reported. Bombed out homes were often looted – many notorious criminals of the post-war era got started on their life of crime under cover of the wartime black-out.

The population was subjected to a never-ending government propaganda campaign designed to keep attention focused on the war effort. People were warned not to talk about any war work they might be involved in or any information they might have concerning shipping, airfields or the deployment of the armed forces. 'Careless Talk Costs Lives' they were reminded. The Ministry of Agriculture told them 'Dig for Victory'. The Ministry of Fuel and Power nagged them not to waste energy, 'Five pounds of coal saved by 1,500,000 homes will provide enough fuel to build a destroyer' they were told. Unnecessary food imports put at risk the lives of merchant seamen so nothing must go to waste. The poster and cartoon character called 'The Squander Bug' tempted the public to spend money rather than buy warbonds, and he was to be resisted.

Alongside the official propaganda was the influence of culture and mass entertainment. Despite long working hours, bombing and the black-out, mass entertainment boomed in the 1940s. By 1945, there were 10 million private radio sets and the BBC not only provided news, information and serious discussion but comedy shows, music and light entertainment. Popular shows like *Workers' Playtime* were broadcast from different factories around the country. The BBC started the war badly, by cancelling most entertainment programmes, but soon learned its lesson and matched the national mood perfectly. The BBC undeniably had a 'good war', having a massive influence on morale. Dance music was very popular, particularly to the sound of 'big bands', both on radio and in the crowded dance halls.

Fig. 5 *Second World War poster urging civilians to save fuel for the war effort*

The cinema also had a golden age, with attendances averaging around 30 million a week. This applied both to British-made films and to Hollywood imports. The film industry was very ready to cooperate with the war effort, both indirectly, by making entertaining films to keep people happy, and directly, through documentary films and feature films calculated to carry the right messages. This was not only through films about the war. In addition to the war films, naval epics and spy thrillers, there were also escapist comedies, uplifting dramas and 'family films' like *Meet Me In St Louis* starring the young Judy Garland.

The popularity of Hollywood films was only one aspect of the extensive American influences on life in Britain. After the United States entered the war in December 1941, it was natural that the allies should project favourable images of each other as part of the common war effort. By 1943, there were increasingly large numbers of American servicemen based in Britain as allied forces prepared for the liberation of Europe. This brought Americans and Britons into contact with each other in ways that had never happened before.

A closer look

American influences on wartime Britain

American influences on Britain in the 1940s were not new. But the war brought a sudden influx of American soldiers (often known as 'GIs' from the term General Infantry) into many areas, such as East Anglia and Lancashire. There were close contacts between American troops and local people. Despite the popular saying that the 'Yanks' were 'over-paid, over-sexed and over-here', relations with British civilians were generally good, leading to many lasting friendships. One effect was the number of 'GI brides' – the 60,000 British girls who married American soldiers and moved to the United States

Activity

Feature films and the Second World War

There are hundreds of films giving interesting glimpses of what Britain was like during the war – or at least what it was supposed to be like. Try to find:

- *Went The Day Well?* – a film about English villagers taking on a secret German invasion
- *Mrs Miniver* – a film about a gallant British housewife coping with the Blitz
- Laurence Olivier's *Henry V*, making a parallel between Britain in 1944 and Shakespeare's version of the Battle of Agincourt in 1415.

Fig. 6 *Integration not segregation. Inter-racial mixing on the dance floor. Black American GIs found discrimination based on colour less of a problem in Britain than in the United States*

after the war. The mixing of American troops with local girls often caused local jealousies.

These social contacts helped to spread North American cultural influences. Music, dance, food and language became more Americanised. The 'big-band' sound associated with the American Glenn Miller, the 'jive' and the 'jitterbug' took over British dance halls. American luxuries such as Lucky Strike cigarettes, chewing gum, or nylon stockings were desirable in the eyes of British people used to rationing. Even casual phrases like 'OK' marked the pervasiveness of American influence.

There was much genuine enthusiasm for the American Way. Some people, however, resented the higher pay of the American troops as well as their access to goods which were unavailable to the locals. There was some dislike of the colour discrimination which the Americans imposed on their troops and tried to impose on pubs, dance halls and cinemas frequented by Americans. Several violent incidents occurred over this. In the main, however, British people had a favourable image of their American allies, and these positive attitudes continued into the post-war era.

Summing up the impact on attitudes by 1945

It is difficult to reach definitive judgements about the impact of the Second World War on attitudes of people in Britain. The social history of the war was in fact millions of different histories, young and old, men and women, soldiers and civilians, town and country, north and south. Any attempt to reach a balanced overall conclusion will be full of exceptions and contradictions. But trying to reach such conclusions is what historians have to do.

Activity

Revision exercise

Make a summary chart like the one below, analysing the impact of the 1939–45 war in terms of losses and gains for civilians.

Areas of impact	Losses	Gains
Work life		
Home life		
Housing		
Children		
Women		
Men		
Personal freedom		
Health		
Social life		

There is a genuine debate about the extent to which the Second World War broke down class barriers and increased equality in Britain. On the one hand, it is claimed that there was a fundamental shift in public attitudes, demanding greater fairness in society, and that this shift proved lasting. It is argued that there was a 'post-war consensus' after 1945 that influenced the policies of all the major parties towards a classless society. On the other hand, it can be convincingly argued that such ideas about equality merely dented class divisions but did not break them; and that any 'social revolution' caused by the impact of war was only temporary anyway.

There were certainly big changes in attitudes towards government and politics. The war transformed the image of the monarchy, which had been badly damaged by the Abdication Crisis in 1936. Between 1939 and 1945, not least because of the favourable impression created by the two young princesses, Elizabeth and Margaret Rose, the royal family became a focal point for national unity. The war also strengthened links between Britain and the empire and commonwealth. The prime ministers of Australia, Canada and South Africa, Robert Menzies, Mackenzie King and J. C. Smuts, worked closely with Churchill and were widely admired in Britain.

Attitudes towards the Labour Party and its leadership also changed decisively. Before the war, many of these leaders were virtually unknown to the wider public; it was also quite easy to attack them as revolutionary socialists, and unpatriotic. After the work of men like Attlee and Bevin in the wartime coalition government, such ideas were plainly nonsense. Labour politicians had proved themselves to be reliable and effective, closely associated with a whole range of popular domestic policies. Labour also benefited from the legacies of the past. Memories of the Great Depression of the 1930s were still raw in 1945. As a result of the war, people were much readier to accept planning and government intervention. The idea of 'never again' was already deeply rooted long before the Labour Party adopted it as a campaign slogan for the 1945 general election.

Assessment of attitudes towards wider social trends is less clear cut. Many people had their lives utterly changed by the war – but many did not. Many people wanted the changes brought by war to continue into peacetime – many did not. Some of the propaganda images that were burned into the national consciousness in the war years closely matched real-life experiences – but such images also concealed unpleasant truths people preferred not to think about. Distinguishing myths from realities can be difficult, because when people looked back at the war years after the war was over many of them remembered the myths they had been led to believe in, not what actually happened. Not everybody liked eating Spam, or listening to Vera Lynn singing about the white cliffs of Dover, or putting up with shortages while being told not to grumble about them.

However, it would be wrong to believe that the British people were somehow subjected to mass brainwashing. However brilliant Churchill's speeches were, however cunning and pervasive the official propaganda was, they could never have had the effect they did unless they were perceived as being at least close to the truth by most of the people, most of the time.

■ **Cross-reference**

The **Abdication Crisis** is outlined on page 91.

Summary questions

1 How far was British society changed by the experiences of the Second World War?

2 How far did the various sections of British society make the sacrifices required for the national war effort?

The Attlee governments, 1945–51: economic crisis and recovery

In this chapter you will learn about:

- why Labour won the 1945 general election so decisively

- the causes and extent of the economic crisis facing Britain immediately after the Second World War

- the economic policies of the Labour governments between 1945 and 1951

- how far economic recovery had been achieved by 1951.

All our enemies having surrendered unconditionally, or being about to do so, I was instantly dismissed by the British electorate.

1 *Winston Churchill commenting on his defeat in the 1945 general election*

To-day may rightly be regarded as 'D-Day' in the Battle of the New Britain.

2 *From a speech by John Freeman, Labour MP for Watford, House of Commons, 16 August 1945*

In 1945, the election result represented a genuine turning point in British politics. It came as a bitter disappointment to the man who had 'won the war', Winston Churchill. Not only Churchill himself but also most of the rest of the world failed to understand the landslide victory for Labour; a victory that meant Labour was able, for the first time, to form a government with an overall majority. When Labour MPs took their seats in the newly-elected House of Commons, they outnumbered their Conservative opponents by two to one. For a party which had suffered deep party divisions and a disastrous electoral defeat in 1931, and had won only 154 seats in the 1935 election, it was a stunning comeback.

Question

Churchill found it hard to understand what had gone wrong. Can you explain why he was surprised?

Table 1 *Results of the 1945 general election*

Party	Seats won	% seats won	Votes (million)	% of the vote
Conservatives	197	31.0	9.10	36.2
Cons and allies*	209	32.7	9.97	39.6
Labour	393	61.0	11.96	48.2
Liberals	12	0.02	2.25	9.0

From Thorpe, A., **Britain in the Era of the Two World Wars**, *1994*

*National Liberals and Northern Ireland Unionists

Cross-reference

Bevin and **Morrison** are profiled on pages 101 and 102, and **Cripps** on page 77. **Hugh Dalton** is introduced on page 122.

Attlee's government remained in power until 1951. It was a very stable team, with remarkably few changes at the top. The key personalities were Attlee himself, Ernest Bevin as Foreign Secretary, Herbert Morrison as Leader in the House of Commons, Hugh Dalton as Chancellor and Stafford Cripps at the Board of Trade. The Labour government had great ambitions to transform Britain, through the nationalisation and revitalising of industry and through building a new 'welfare state'. But the government also inherited major problems, both in the economy and in Britain's expensive overseas commitments. Historians are still divided about the achievements of Attlee's government. For some, Labour managed to push through most of its reforms in the face of colossal economic difficulties; for others, it was a story of muddled priorities and missed opportunities.

The reasons for the 'Labour landslide' in 1945

Fig. 1 *Cartoon by Illingworth, July 1945 on the election result. Umpire John Bull (i.e. the British voter) changes bowler. Clement Attlee was a keen cricket fan*

Fig. 2 *Clement Attlee with victory smile, after winning his seat in the Limehouse division of Stepney. Attlee not only won his seat but defeated Winston Churchill to bring the Labour Party into power, 26 July 1945*

The 1945 general election and its result

Although Winston Churchill had wanted to continue the wartime coalition until the war against Japan ended, the Labour Party had rejected this on the grounds that there had been no general election for 10 years. On 23 May, therefore, the Churchill war coalition had formerly ended, although Churchill had remained as head of a 'caretaker' government until the general election in July. Few people knew how the 1945 election might turn out, because party politics had been pushed into the background for so long. When the election came, it brought a stunning surprise. The 1945 election brought an end to the Conservative dominance of government which went back to 1931. For Labour, it was the culmination of a 50-year struggle to win an overall majority in the House of Commons.

Barbara Castle was a young Labour MP in 1945. Dalton was a Labour MP who had served in the 1940–5 wartime coalition government.

> Despite the euphoria of the campaign, no one in the Labour Party, except Aneurin Bevan, believed that the party could snatch victory from the wartime Prime Minister... Then on the 26th July the news broke in an astonished press: Labour was in an overall majority.

3   *From Castle, B., Fighting All the Way, 1993*

> The country went to the polls on July 5th. Hopes were rising amongst Labour supporters but I could not persuade myself that Labour could have won more than about 280 seats. On this result there would be a small Tory majority. My own result was successful and compared with 1935 my majority was up, but by less than a thousand votes. Taken across the country this would not have produced a Labour majority. But soon news came through from other constituencies and this lifted hopes sky high. The final result gave Labour a large overall majority of 152 seats.

4   *From Dalton, H., The Fateful Years: Memoirs 1931–1945, 1957*

Exploring the detail

The end of the war against Japan

On 7 May 1945, the German High Command surrendered unconditionally to the allies. The European war was over although war against Japan continued. Japan finally surrendered initially on 15 August, and formally on 2 September 1945.

Activity

Source analysis

Study the comments by Barbara Castle and Hugh Dalton in Sources 3 and 4. Using these sources and other evidence in this chapter, explain why the 1945 election result came as such a surprise to Castle and Dalton.

5 Conclusion

The extent of change in Britain between 1906 and 1951

It is easy to identify many aspects in which there was significant change in Britain between 1906 and 1951. In 1906, Britain was a great empire, an undisputed world power. By 1951, after going through two world wars and the Great Depression, Britain was struggling to cope with economic burdens at home and abroad. In the new post-war world, the age of the European powers was over and the age of the new American and Soviet superpowers had begun. Britain's imperial decline was symbolised by the events of 1947, with the decision to withdraw from India, and the humiliating dependence upon financial aid from the United States.

There had also been a political transformation. In 1906, the Labour Party had only recently come into existence and had achieved its first limited electoral breakthrough, with a mere 29 seats; for Labour to form a government was absolutely unthinkable. The Liberal Party had swept to power with an enormous majority and regarded itself as a natural party of government. By 1951, Labour had held power in a majority government for a full parliamentary term. Even in defeat in 1951, Labour remained a mass party with a huge popular vote. The Liberals were now almost obliterated as a political force, reduced to six MPs.

There had also been considerable social change. In 1906, working in domestic service was the most common single source of employment in Britain. Much of the country was made up of the landed estates owned by the aristocracy and gentry. By 1951, many aristocratic families were facing bankruptcy, forced to open their stately homes to coach loads of day visitors in order to get by. Britain both seemed to be and actually was a more egalitarian society, with more openings for education and personal advancement for ordinary people.

Britain looked a changed society by 1951. Many more people regarded themselves as belonging to the middle classes. They owned motor cars, lived in suburban houses, took regular holidays. There were wider leisure opportunities. Radio and cinema had become part and parcel of the social life of the nation. Patterns of employment had changed, especially during the two wars. By 1951, the impact of the NHS and Labour's welfare reforms was already beginning to have an effect on the nation's health and wellbeing.

It is also true that people in Britain believed, and wanted to believe, that the society they lived in had been greatly changed for the better. In 1951, there was still pride in having won the war, and a strong belief that the wartime sacrifices had been for a good purpose, making Britain a fairer society and bringing people together. Nobody wished to return to the 1930s. People convinced themselves that Britain had made a decisive change for the better.

Yet, it would be a mistake to exaggerate the speed and extent of social transformation between 1906 and 1951. There were countless ways in which there was continuity with the past. The political system was much as before. The monarchy had survived the Abdication Crisis of 1936 and had kept the respect and loyalty of the vast majority of people. The war had actually strengthened the monarchy considerably, with the royal family constantly seen on newsreels. The war had also strengthened links with the commonwealth. All this was demonstrated by the mass popular celebrations of the coronation of Queen Elizabeth II in 1953.

Despite the constitutional crisis of 1910–11, the House of Lords was little different in 1951 than when Edward VII was king. Hereditary peers still wore their ermine robes and went through the old-fashioned routines handed down by past generations. There was no serious attempt to alter the fundamental structure of the British constitution – not until the 1990s with Tony Blair's attempt to reform the Lords, and the devolution of powers from Westminster to Scotland and Wales.

In education, R.A. Butler's 1944 Education Act aimed to bring about significant change – but there was no revolution. The influence of the private, fee-paying schools remained pervasive. The path to the top of British society and politics still went through schools like Eton to the 'best' colleges at Oxford and Cambridge, and from there to parliament, or the diplomatic service, or the professions.

Seen from the standpoint of the early 21st century (or even of Americans at the time), Britain did not appear to be all that 'modern' in 1951. The North–South divide was still apparent. Few people except the privileged travelled abroad. The most popular programmes on the radio were traditional comedy shows and the safe and respectable serial *Mrs Dale's Diary*. (The fact that in 2008 *The Archers* is still going strong on radio while *Coronation Street* remains a staple of ITV tells you something about social continuity.)

Britain was a country where everything was seen in black and white. The films seen in the cinema were mostly black and white, so were the photos in family albums. People mostly wore black. The buildings were black – whatever the natural colour of the bricks or stone they were originally built with, air pollution turned them all the same sooty black. There were other forms of air pollution. Britain in 1951 still had deep, foul-smelling fogs as bad as anything in Victorian London. It was impossible to see clearly across the top deck of any bus, or any pub, or any school staffroom because of the permanent cloud of blue smoke from all those cigarettes.

Despite political and social changes and all the officially-encouraged 'togetherness' during the Second World War, class divisions were still entrenched. The class of a person was easy to recognise by their accent, or their dress, or the house they lived in, or the job they did. Grammar schools allowed some degree of social mobility but, as a general rule, grammar school places went to middle-class children. Britain still had many awful slums in 1951, though local authorities were beginning to move ahead with slum clearance schemes and building new 'overspill' towns outside the cities.

In many respects, then, the gap between present-day Britain and the Britain of 1951 was wider than any differences between 1951 and 1906. Yet, it is difficult to reach definitive conclusions about social change. Whatever historians might say, few people attending the Festival of Britain in 1951 would have accepted the view that things had not changed much from 1906. Exactly how much changed, and precisely why remains a very good question.

Did you know?

Festival of Britain

The main centre of this national Festival was on London's South Bank, but celebrations were held all over the country. Not only did it mark a hundred years since the Great Exhibition of 1851, but also the end of the post-war era. The Festival looked both to Britain's past and future. Though a popular attraction, it provoked controversy. To some it was a reward for years of austerity, to others a frivolous waste of money.

Bibliography

Britain 1906 –51

Students

Benson, T. (2007) *The Cartoon Century*, Random House.

Cawood, I. (2004) *Britain in the Twentieth Century*, Routledge.

Hunt, J. and Watson, S. (1990) *Britain and the Two World Wars*, Cambridge University Press.

Mayer, A. (2002) *Women in Britain 1900–2000*, Hodder & Stoughton.

Murphy, D. (ed.) (2000) *Britain 1914–2000*, HarperCollins.

Petheram, L. (2001) *Britain in the 20th Century*, Nelson Thornes.

Roberts, M. (2001) *Britain 1846–1964: The Challenge of Change*, Oxford University Press.

Rowe, C. (2004) *Britain 1929–1998*, Heinemann.

See also the many very useful articles in Modern History Review on this period.

Teachers and extension

Adelman, P. (1999) *The Rise of the Labour Party 1880–1945*, Longman.

Ball, S. (1995) *The Conservative Party and British Politics 1902–1951*, Longman.

Black, J. (2000) *Modern British History Since 1900*, Macmillan.

Bruley, S. (1999) *Women in Britain Since 1900*, London.

Charmley, J. (1999) *The Conservative Party, 1900–1986*, London.

Clarke, P. (1996) *Hope and Glory: Britain 1900–1990*, Penguin.

Hirst, D. (1999) *Welfare and Society, 1832–1991*, London.

Johnson, P. (ed.) (1994) *20th Century Britain: Economic, Social and Cultural Change*, Pearson.

May, T. (1995) *An Economic and Social History of Britain 1760–1990*, Longman.

Pearce, M. and Stewart, G, (2002) *British Political History 1867–2001*, Routledge.

Pearce, R. (2003) *Contemporary Britain 1914–1979*, Longman.

Pope, R. (1991) *War and Society in Britain 1899–1948*, Longman.

Seaman, L. C. B. (1966) *Post-Victorian Britain 1902–1951*, Methuen.

Shinwell, E. (1973) *I've Lived Through It All*, Victor Gollancz.

Simpson, W. O. (1986) *Changing Horizons, Britain 1914–80*, Stanley Thornes.

Stevenson, J. (1990) *British Society 1914–45*, Penguin.

Taylor, A. J. P. (2001) *English History 1914–1945*, Oxford Paperbacks.

Williams, F. (1961) *A Prime Minister Remembers*, Heinemann.

Section 1 Britain 1906–18

Students

Byrne, M. (2005) *Britain 1895–1918*, Hodder Murray.

Rees, R. (2003) *Britain 1890–1939*, Heinemann.

Teachers and extension

Adelman, P. (1996) *Great Britain And The Irish Question 1800–1922*, Hodder & Stoughton.

Bartley, P. (1998) *Votes for Women 1860–1928*, Hodder & Stoughton.

Marwick, A. (1967) *The Deluge*, Bodley Head.

Pugh, M. (1988) *Lloyd George*, Longman.

Pugh, M. (1982) *The Making of Modern British Politics*, Blackwell.

Novels and memoirs

Brittain, V. (1978) *Testament of Youth*, Gollancz.

Section 2 Britain 1918–29

Students

Pearce, R. (2000) *Britain: Domestic Politics 1918–1939*, Hodder & Stoughton.

Pearce, R. (1992) *Britain: Industrial Relations and the Economy*, Hodder & Stoughton.

Pope, R. (1998) *The British Economy Since 1914*, Longman.

Teachers and extension

Adelman, P. (1981) *The Decline of the Liberal Party 1900–1931*, Longman.

Morgan, K. O. (1981) *David Lloyd George*, University of Wales Press.

Mowat, C. L. (1962) *Britain between the Wars 1918–1940*, Methuen.

Skidelsky, R. (1967) *Politicians and the Slump*, Macmillan.

Stevenson, J. and Cook, C. (1994) *Britain in the Depression*, Longman.

Section 3 Britain 1929–40

Students

Pearce, R. (1992) *Britain: Domestic Politics 1918–1939*, Hodder & Stoughton.

Teachers and extension

Branson, N. and Heinemann, M. (1973) *Britain in the Nineteen Thirties*, Panther.

Constantine, S. (1982) *Unemployment in Britain between the Wars*, Longman.

Mowat, C. L. (1962) *Britain between the Wars 1918–1940*, Methuen.

Watts, D. (1996) *Baldwin and the Search for Consensus*, Hodder & Stoughton.

Novels, plays, films and memoirs

Breadline: The Great Depression at Home (1996) Episode 13 of *People's Century*.

Greenwood, W. (1993) *Love on the Dole*, Vintage.

Orwell, G. (1937) *The Road to Wigan Pier*, Penguin.

Priestley, J. B. (1934) *English Journey*, Heinemann.

Woodruff, W. (2002) *The Road to Nab End*, Abacus.

Woodruff, W. (2003) *Beyond Nab End*, Abacus.

Section 4 Britain 1940–51

Students

Adelman, P. (2005) *Britain: Domestic Politics 1939–64*, Hodder & Stoughton.

Jefferys, K. (1992) *The Attlee Government 1945–1951*, Longman.

Jenkins, A. (1977) *The Forties*, Heinemann.

Pearce, R. (1994) *Attlee's Labour governments 1945–51*, Routledge.

Teachers and extension

Addison, P. (1989) *The Road to 1945*, Jonathan Cape.

Best, G. (2005) *Churchill: A Study in Greatness*, London.

Calder, A. (1992) *The People's War*, Pimlico.

Charmley, J. (1993) *Churchill: The End of Glory*, Hodder & Stoughton.

Childs, D. (1992) *Britain Since 1945*, Routledge.

Goodman, S. (2005) *Children of War*, John Murray.

Hennessy, P. (1988) *Never Again: Britain 1945–1951*, Macmillan.

Hennessy, P. (2000) *The Prime Minister: The Office and its Holders since 1945*, Penguin.

Jenkins, R. (2001) *Churchill*, Pan.

Kynaston, D. (2007) *Austerity Britain*, Sutton.

Marr, A. (2007) *Post-war Britain*, BBC Books.

Marwick, A. (1976) *The Home Front*, Thames & Hudson.

Morgan, K. (1984) *Labour In Power 1945–1951*, Oxford University Press.

Tiratsoo, N. (ed.) (1998) *From Blitz to Blair*, Penguin.

Novels

Boorman, J. (1987) *Hope and Glory*, Faber & Faber.

Dobbs, M. (2003) *Winston's War*, HarperCollins.

Dobbs, M. (2005) *Churchill's Hour*, HarperCollins.

Dobbs, M. (2007) *Never Surrender*, Sourcebooks Landmark.

Films

A Diary for Timothy

Homes for the People

Listen to Britain

Mrs Miniver

Went the Day Well?

Websites

www.bbc.co.uk/onthisday/

www.britishpathe.com/

www.churchill-society-london.org.uk/

www.conservativehistory.org.uk/

www.iwm.org.uk/

www.labourhistory.org.uk/

www.liberalhistory.org.uk/

www.nationalarchives.gov.uk/

www.npg.org.uk/

www.spartacus.schoolnet.co.uk/

Use internet search engines to search for past articles/ editorials on the main media/press websites plus images connected with this period.

Acknowledgements

The authors and publisher would like to thank the following for permission to reproduce material:

Source texts:

p8 Extract from 'Liberal election song' composed by S. E. Boyle, quoted in Braham, M., *Southport Liberals 100 Years*, Michael Braham, 1985; p16 Song of the Budget League, sung to the tune of 'Marching through Georgia', From Seaman, R. D. H., *The Reform of the Lords*, Edward Arnold, 1971; p26 Adapted extract from Lloyd George's speech at Limehouse, July 1909. Taken from Royston Pike, E., *Human Documents of the Lloyd George Era*, Allen and Unwin, 1972; p27 Extract from a speech by Lloyd George in 1909. Adapted from speeches quoted in Roberts, M., *Britain 1846–1964*, Oxford University Press, 2001 and Royston Pike, E., *Human Documents of the Lloyd George Era*, Allen and Unwin, 1972; p34 'The General', Siegfried Sassoon, From arrangement by Hart-Davis, R., *The War Poems of Siegfried Sassoon*, Faber and Faber, 1983; p45 Adapted from Naomi Loughnan's account of munition work in Marlow, J. (ed.), *The Virago Book of Women and the Great War*, Virago, 1998; p48 (Fig. 1) From a speech by D. Lloyd George, quoted in *The Concise Dictionary of Quotations*, Collins, 1986; p54 (top) Stanley Baldwin MP speaking at the Carlton Club meeting. Quoted in Young, G. M., *Stanley Baldwin*, Rupert Hart-Davis, 1952; p54 (centre) Bonar Law, the Conservative leader, speaking about Lloyd George at the Carlton Club meeting. Quoted in Pearce, R., *Britain: Domestic Politics 1918–39*, Hodder & Stoughton, 2005; p54 (bottom) Winston Churchill, in a speech in 1945. Quoted in Jones, T., *Lloyd George*, Oxford University Press, 1951; p65 Anti-MacDonald election song, 1931. Quoted in Pearce, M. and Stewart, G., *British Political History*, 3rd edition, Routledge, 2002; p72 (top) Shinwell, E., *I've Lived Through It All*, Victor Gollancz Ltd, 1973; p72 (bottom) Adapted from Snowden, P., *The Autobiography of Philip Snowden*, Volume Two, Nicholson and Watson Ltd, 1934; p78 'Moving Through the Silent Crowd' by Stephen Spender. Quoted in Brett, M. (ed.), *New Collected Poems of Stephen Spender*, Faber & Faber, 2004; p79

Taylor, A. J. P., *English History 1914–1945*, Penguin, 1970; p97 (top) Adapted from Churchill, W. S., *The Gathering Storm*, Cassell, 1948; p97 (bottom) Adapted from the *Diary of Lord Halifax* quoted in Gilbert, M., *Winston S. Churchill, Finest Hour*, Houghton Mifflin Company, 1983; p98 Extract from Churchill's first speech as prime minister, 13 May 1940. Quoted in Jenkins, R., *Churchill*, Pan Books, 2001; p99 (top) Extract from Churchill's speech, 18 June 1940. Quoted in Jenkins, R., *Churchill*, Pan Books, 2001; p99 (bottom) Quoted in Charmley, J., *Churchill: the End of Glory*, Hodder & Stoughton, 1993; p109 (bottom) From a report in the *Middlesbrough Evening Gazette*, 3 February 1942; p120 (top) Winston Churchill commenting on his defeat in the 1945 general election. Quoted in Pearce, R., *Attlee's Labour Governments 1945–51*, Routledge, 1994; p121 (top) From Castle, B., *Fighting All the Way*, Macmillan, 1993; p121 (bottom) From Dalton, H., *The Fateful Years: Memoirs 1931–1945*, Frederick Muller, 1957; p128 Adapted from Dalton, H., *High Tide and After: Memoirs 1945–1960*, Frederick Muller, 1957

Photographs courtesy of:

Anne Ronan Picture Library pp13 (top), 23, 25, 59, 88, 115; Larry Burrows/Time Life Pictures/Getty Images p136; Cartoon museum p107; Central Press/Getty Images p27; Edimedia Art Archive pp38, 41 (bottom); Gallagher Memorial Library, Glasgow Caledonian University Special Collections and Archives p87; Getty Images ppiv, 124; The Lordprice Collection/HIP/Topfoto p113; Edward G Malindine/Getty Images p137; Photo by Felix Man/Picture Post/Hulton Archive/Getty Images p118; Public Domain pp10, 36, 83; solosyndication.com p121 (left); Topfoto pp9, 12, 14, 69, 72, 78, 90, 94, 104, 110, 117, 121 (right), 127, 129, 132, 141; Topfoto/English Heritage/HIP p85; World History Archive pp8, 13 (bottom), 17 (top and bottom), 18, 22, 28, 30, 34, 39 , 41 (top), 44, 45, 46, 48, 49, 55, 56, 61, 65, 75, 76, 81, 92, 97, 98, 101, 114

Cover photograph: courtesy of Getty Images

Photo Research by www.uniquedimension.com

Index